MISSISSIPPI
LEGENDS & LORE

MISSISSIPPI
LEGENDS & LORE

Alan Brown

THE
History
PRESS

Published by The History Press
Charleston, SC
www.historypress.com

Front cover, top left: Wikimedia Commons; *top center*: Wikimedia Commons; *top right*: Wikimedia Commons; *bottom*: author's collection.
Back cover: Wikimedia Commons.

First published 2020

Manufactured in the United States

ISBN 9781467145176

Library of Congress Control Number: 2020938462

To Cade and Owen Walker, who keep me writing.

CONTENTS

CONTENTS

CONTENTS

INTRODUCTION

In the minds of many people who live outside of the South, Mississippi is the representative southern state. When I asked myself why this is, the diverse makeup of its people, its geography and its history seemed to be the obvious answer. To a greater or lesser extent, most of the southern states share these features with Mississippi. However, the primary reason probably lies in the creativity of Mississippi's people. While other southern states can lay claim to specific musical traditions, only Mississippi has the Delta, the birthplace of the blues, and Jimmie Rodgers, the father of country music. Mississippians also excel at storytelling. Some of its published authors, like William Faulkner, Eudora Welty, Richard Wright, Willie Morris, John Grisham and Greg Iles, have achieved international fame. Storytelling also flows in the blood of average Mississippians, as is evidenced by the rich body of legends that has sprung from the Magnolia State.

The state of Mississippi is a prime breeding ground for legends, owing to the wide variety of cultures that have lived here. The Woodland and Mississippian cultures left behind their burial and ceremonial mounds, beginning around AD 950. The Chickasaw and Choctaw tribes who followed were descendants of the Mississippian culture. The arrival of French colonists in April 1699 ushered in the colonial era at Fort Maurepas in present-day Ocean Springs. Under the leadership of Pierre Le Moyne d'Iberville, the French established "New France" in the Natchez area. In the eighteenth century, Mississippi was governed by the Spanish, French and British. Slaves were transported to Mississippi by the colonists who settled there. Mississippi was open for settlement by Europeans following the signing of the Treaty of Dancing Rabbit in 1830, when the Choctaws were removed to reservations in Oklahoma on the Trail of Tears. By 1850, 55 percent of Mississippi's total population was African American. However, because of the Great Migration between 1916 and 1970, Africans Americans became a minority in Mississippi after the 1930s. All of these different ethnic and racial groups have contributed to Mississippi's lore. The Choctaw legend of the "little people" and the African American tale of Robert Johnson's deal with the devil are good examples.

Mississippi's geography has also contributed to the stories that people have told for centuries. Most of the state consists of low hills as part of the East Gulf Coastal Plain. The most fertile soil is found in the northeast part of the state. The Mississippi Delta in the northwest benefits from silt deposited by the flooding of the Mississippi River. Mississippi's rivers—the Pascagoula River, the Pearl River, the Yazoo River, the Tombigbee River and the Big Black River—have served as important waterways for centuries. Large bays can be found along the coastline. In the Mississippi Sound are a number of islands, such as Cat Island, Deer Island, Round Island, Petit Bois Island, Horn Island and East and West Ship Islands. The landscape is an important component in many of the legends because of the people's close connection to the land. Tales dealing with farming, such as the murder of Janie Sharp in Rural Hill, and with the sea, such as the exploits of the pirate Patrick Scott, are told throughout the state and beyond.

Finally, Mississippi's violent past resonates through the state's legends and folktales. The brutal treatment of African Americans held in slavery in the eighteenth and nineteenth centuries, as well as the mistreatment of black people under the Jim Crow laws in the twentieth century, left an indelible impact on the state's history and culture. The carnage and suffering caused by the Civil War battles fought in Mississippi—the Sieges of Vicksburg and Corinth, the Battle of Champion Hill, the Battle of Brice's Cross Roads and the Battle of Raymond—are also memorialized in the lore of the state. The destruction wrought by natural catastrophes, such as Hurricane Camille in 1969 and Hurricane Katrina in 2005, has left indelible imprints on the state's landscape, architecture, history and stories. Stories about King's Tavern in Natchez and the Amos Deason Home in Ellisville are reflections of Mississippi's past, which William Faulkner wrote in *Requiem for a Nun* "is never dead. It's not even past."

A strong connection exists between the mysteries and legends included in this collection. The appearance of strange creatures that defy identification, like the Mississippi Wild Man, becomes an important part of the population's collective memory, thanks in part to the exposure these sightings are given in the local media. Murderers like Ouida Keeton and Glen Edward Rogers are transformed into legendary figures if the reasons for their crimes are unknown. An aura of mystery has enveloped Mississippi's UFO encounters, like the Pascagoula Alien Abduction, because little evidence has been found beyond the testimony of witnesses. The ghost lore generated by places like King's Tavern in Natchez and Merrehope continue to tantalize our imaginations because they raise the question, "Could such things really happen?" The fate of people like Jacqueline Levitz in Vicksburg and Janie Sharp in Rural Hill will remain part of Mississippi's lore for a long time because they add another element of mystery to the most mysterious stage of human life: death. One could say that we love to share mysteries and legends because they give us the opportunity to explain the unexplainable.

This compilation is only a fraction of the legends that either initially existed in the oral form or have become part of the oral tradition after appearing in print. Of course, the legends themselves will continue to evolve as the tellers continue to add their own embellishments or make their own deletions. Consequently, legends will never supplant the historical record. Their value lies in the extent to which they embody the hopes, fears and awe of the people who generated them.

1
CIVIL WAR LEGENDS

THE AMOS DEASON HOUSE'S BLOODY PAST
(ELLISVILLE)

Ed Chapman began construction of his French Raised Cottage in Jones County in the 1830s. Chapman died before the house was finished; Boyles McManus completed construction of the house in 1845. The first occupants of the house and the seven-hundred-acre homestead were Amos and Eleanor Deason. For the most part, the Amos Deason House is a typical mid-nineteenth-century southern home. The builder employed a technique to make the exterior appear to have been made of stone. The hexagonal-shaped vestibule opens into the porch. The hand-hewn pin timber and the weatherboards were connected using wooden pegs. The interlocking wooden shake shingles were hand-split. All of the rooms are connected to the wraparound porch, which figures prominently into the Amos Deason House's most notorious episode.

The hauntings at the Amos Deason House date to the Civil War. Unlike most of the citizens of Mississippi, the residents of Jones County, as a whole, were not in favor of separating from the union, and they instructed their delegate to the secession convention in Jackson to vote against withdrawing from the nation. However, the delegate disregarded his orders and voted with the secessionists. Consequently, a large number of the men of Jones County refused to enlist in the Confederate army until the draft was instituted in 1862. One of these men, Newt Knight, served as a hospital orderly for a

On October 3, 1863, Confederate deserter Newton Knight shot and killed Major Amos McLemore inside the Amos Deason House. *Author's collection.*

while. However, he deserted after the Confederacy passed a law permitting any man who owned twenty or more slaves to avoid the draft. Convinced that this was "a rich man's war and a poor man's fight," he and his band of followers returned to Jones County and hid in caves deep in the swamps of the Leaf River. Within a few weeks, Knight's renegade army swelled to over one hundred deserters, who periodically left their hideout—known as "Devil's Den"—to visit their families and work on their farms. Still, most of the people of Jones County considered Knight's band to be nothing more than criminals unworthy of safe harbor. In fact, some accused Knight's men of robbing trains headed to and from Mobile.

By 1863, the Confederacy was determined to capture Knight's army. Major Amos McLemore, a native of Jones County, was dispatched to scour the swamps for the renegades after the Confederate army failed to apprehend them. Because of the increased pressure exerted by McLemore and his men, Knight decided that his nemesis had to die. Knight made his move on October 3, 1863. Having received word that McLemore was staying at the Amos Deason House, Knight and two of his men approached the house under the cover of darkness. Knight peered through the bedroom window and identified McLemore as the man standing in front of the fireplace, but he was unable to take a clear shot. Taking a deep breath, Knight threw the bedroom door open and shot McLemore point blank. The stricken man screamed, "I'm killed!" and fell to the floor. Amid the confusion, Knight and his comrades managed to slip out of the house and return to the swamp. McLemore died from his wound two days later.

In 1991, descendants of Amos Deason presented the historic structure to the local chapter of the Daughters of the American Revolution (DAR). After restoring the house, the ladies opened it up to the public. Not surprisingly, many visitors to the home inquire about its haunted history. The best-known ghost story concerns the spot in the bedroom where McLemore fell to the floor. The brutal murder, people say, is memorialized on the bedroom floor where he fell. Amos Deason's wife, Eleanor, attempted to remove the bloodstains from the floor, but they reappeared every time it rained. Legend has it that the servants used sandstones from the nearby creek to try to erase the blood, but to no avail. People say that new flooring was placed in the bedroom to cover the stains, but traces of blood were found on the joists supporting the house, suggested that the pool of blood leaked through the floor.

In recent years, other ghost stories have surfaced. For years, a number of DAR members have confessed to being reluctant to stay in the house alone. Some visitors and docents claim to have seen an antique rocking chair rock on its own. One evening, while the DAR members were preparing for a reenactment, the daughter of one of the members was walking through the house wearing an antebellum dress. A television crew covering the event recorded a spectral voice saying, "Get out of my dress!" During an open house, a lamp inexplicably fell off a cabinet. Frances Murphy, president of the Tallahala Chapter of the Daughters of the American Revolution, said that the apparition of a woman has been sighted walking down the hallway. She added that several years ago, schoolchildren saw the faces of ghostly children dressed in old-fashioned clothing staring out of the windows of the Amos Deason House.

In an article published in the *Clarion-Ledger* on October 28, 2014, paranormal investigator Lacey Stringer told reporter Therese Apel that a member of the DAR was changing clothes in the "murder room" when she detected the coppery smell of blood. During an investigation, one of the group's members was pulled out of his chair and onto the floor. Afterward, he said that something had pulled him out of the chair. During their electronic voice phenomena (EVP) sessions, the group recorded the voice of a hysterical woman saying, "Buddy, there's someone up in the attic." In response to the question, "Whose house is this?" a ghost voice replied, "Mine" on the voice recorder. Stringer estimated that five ghosts inhabit the Amos Deason House.

THE IMPREGNATING BULLET (RAYMOND)

One of the strangest lessons produced during the Civil War took the form of a medical mystery. In 1874, Dr. Legrand Cuerry Capers Jr.'s account of a medical miracle that grew to legendary proportions was published in a medical journal titled the *American Medical Weekly*. A graduate of Thomas Jefferson University at Princeton, Dr. Capers practiced medicine as a ship's physician on Vanderbilt's passenger steamships until 1862. For the remainder of the war, he served as a surgeon in the Fourth Georgia Volunteer Infantry and in Cutshaw's Battalion. In his article, Dr. Capers reported an incident that he claimed to have witnessed during the Battle of Raymond on May 12, 1863. Capers wrote that he was with a company of soldiers that had fallen back to within 150 yards of a house when one of the soldiers staggered a few yards and collapsed. At the same time, Capers heard a piercing scream from the house. He immediately dropped to the ground and diagnosed the young man's injuries. A minié ball had clearly struck the boy in the leg and then ricocheted upward, penetrating the scrotum and removing his left testicle. While Dr. Capers was dressing the boy's wounds, a matronly woman stepped out of the house and begged him to go to one of her daughters, who had been seriously wounded just a few minutes before. Dr. Capers entered the house and rushed to the seventeen-year-old girl's bedside. She had been struck in the lower abdomen by what appeared to have been a minié ball, which left a jagged wound. He only had time to prescribe anodyne before joining the regiment in its retreat.

Six months later, when the Confederate army returned to Raymond, Dr. Capers paid a call on the young woman who had been shot in the stomach. He was shocked to find that her abdomen was greatly enlarged. He was reluctant to state his suspicion that the girl was pregnant, because he was personally acquainted with the girl and his family, whom he knew to be people of high standing. He told the ladies that he was not ready to deliver a conclusive diagnosis and returned to the army, determined to check in on the girl periodically. Then, 278 days after the girl was shot, Dr. Capers delivered her

One of the many artifacts housed at the Old Courthouse Museum is the bullet that was said to have impregnated a young woman after passing through the groin of a soldier. *Author's collection.*

of an eight-pound boy. Examining the child, he discovered something hard inside the baby's scrotum. He operated and removed a flattened minié ball.

Not surprisingly, the story of the "bullet pregnancy" generated a firestorm of publicity. However, two weeks later, in a subsequent issue of the journal, the editor exposed the article as hoax. Dr. Capers, the writer said, "disclaims responsibility for the truth of that impregnation by a Minnie ball, as reported in No. 19 of this Journal." For some reason, though, the general public ignored the truth and clung to the myth, which was generally accepted as medical fact until 1959. However, the legend was revived in a letter published in a "Dear Abby" column in 1982. The writer claimed that she had read the story in a December 1971 edition of *American Heritage* magazine.

This amazing—but totally apocryphal—tale received a second life in the form of a motion picture filmed in Mississippi. Titled *Son of a Gun*, the film was written and directed by Travis Mills, who is based in Brookhaven. Several of the actors were recruited from Hattiesburg. The battle scenes were filmed in Raymond, but most of the movie was shot in and around Port Gibson.

THE GHOSTS OF BEAUVOIR (BILOXI)

Beauvoir, the beautiful ocean-side mansion that will be forever identified with Confederate president Jefferson Davis, was built as a summer home in Biloxi, Mississippi, between 1850 and 1852 by a wealthy planter named James Brown. Beauvoir is an eight-room raised cottage erected on a foundation of massive brick pillars to allow floodwaters from the Gulf of Mexico to flow only through the first floor. To ensure that the house would be comfortable in the summer, Brown designed it with high ceilings, wide porches and large windows. The design also included two small cottages and several outbuildings, such as a brick kitchen. Frank Johnston bought the home in 1873, and he sold it three years later to a wealthy cotton planter from Natchez named Samuel Dorsey. His wife, Sarah Ellis Dorsey, achieved fame as a novelist and historian. In 1877, she invited Jefferson Davis to stay at Beauvoir. During his stay there, Sarah Dorsey assisted him in writing his memoir, *The Rise and Fall of the Confederate Government* (1881). Davis took possession of Beauvoir as a retirement home in 1879. He lived there with his wife, Varina, and his daughter, Varina Anne (known affectionately as "Winnie"), until his death in December 1889. Varina wrote her own book about her husband's life, *Jefferson Davis: A Memoir*, in 1890. In 1891, she and her daughter moved to New York City in the hope of earning a living as writers. Following the death of her daughter in 1898, Varina wanted to sell Beauvoir, but she was concerned that the new buyer would tear it down. In 1902, the United Sons of Confederate Veterans assured her that the house would be preserved by purchasing it and converting it into the Jefferson Davis Soldiers' Home. Over the next few decades, two thousand Confederate veterans and their wives and widows lived in specially built barracks on the property. Around eight hundred of them were laid to rest in the cemetery on the grounds. Today, the Jefferson Davis Shrine has been a museum since 1956. In 2005, Hurricane Katrina did considerable damage to Beauvoir, ripping off the front porch along with part of the slate roof. Some of the antique furnishings were severely damaged by the water, and several columns were washed away. Following the $4 million restoration project, Beauvoir is now, according to director Rick Forte, "as good today as the day they finished it in 1852." The restored beauty of the home may explain why a number of spirits of its former inhabitants have returned.

The most commonly sighted ghosts on the property are the spirits of Jefferson Davis and Varina. For years, tourists have captured the images of Jefferson, Varina and their daughter on film. A number of women who had

Former president of the Confederacy Jefferson Davison lived in this eight-room raised cottage from 1881 until his death in 1899. *Author's collection.*

their bridal portraits taken at Beauvoir claimed that Winnie's ghost could be seen behind them in a window in her room. The best known of these "spirit photographs" was taken in 1984 by Charlie Brock, a Confederate reenactor. His wife and two of her friends posed for a group photograph in front of Beauvoir. After the film was developed, Brock and his wife were shocked by the appearances of two figures in one of the windows. The house had been locked up and closed to visitors at the time.

Members of the Davis family have made their presence known at Beauvoir in other ways as well. In Sylvia Booth Hubbard's book *Ghosts! Personal Accounts of Modern Mississippi Hauntings*, the former superintendent of Beauvoir, Colonel Newton Carr Jr., said that many staff members and visitors witnessed Jefferson Davis's ghost, although he never did: "While I was there, some of the employees said they felt the presence of Mr. Davis. They also said they would see him out of the corner of their eyes, but when they turned to face him, he would disappear." On several occasions, Davis's ghost was mistaken for a reenactor dressed up to look like Davis. The most dramatic paranormal incident at Beauvoir occurred one day when a guest

A woman walking through the garden in back of Beauvoir was told by a ghostly figure resembling Jefferson Davis to get off of his roses. *Author's collection.*

entered the gift shop and complained about the rude behavior of the actor playing Jefferson Davis. Apparently, she had been walking through the rose garden at the time. Rosie, an employee, informed the guest that there were no actors at Beauvoir that day and that "she should listen to Jefferson Davis."

Winnie's ghost has also been known to manifest through sound. Kitsaal Stevens, who works in museum development and programs, said that, one day, a group of seniors were standing on the steps outside of the house when they heard Winnie playing the piano. "The curator was quite adamant at the time not to touch the piano," Stevens said. "Forty seniors turned around and said, 'We're not even in the house!'"

Other spirits appear to be making their presence known as well. Phantom footsteps have been heard walking between the cottages. The strange sound of one set of footsteps suggests that the ghost used a cane; it is possibly the spirit of one of the residents of the Confederate soldiers' home. Colonel Carr said that several of the guards reported seeing the ghosts of Confederate veterans who lived out their final days at Beauvoir. On August 8, 2014, a group of paranormal investigators, Mississippi Gulf Coast

The ghost of a little boy has been seen playing in the Confederate cemetery behind Beauvoir. *Author's collection.*

Paranormal, spent the night at Beauvoir. Their investigation included the cemetery where many of the Confederate veterans were buried. One of the investigators reported feeling cold in the cemetery. During the night, the group experienced a number of spikes on their KII EVP Meter, both inside and outside of the house. Kitsaal Stevens considered the possibility that the ghost of a little boy reported playing in the cemetery was active that night. While standing inside Beauvoir, one member of the group asked the spirits to make a loud noise. Immediately, the investigators heard what sounded like pieces of wood slamming together. The evidence gathered on August 8, 2014, suggests that the hauntings of Beauvoir are of the residual and intelligent variety.

McRAVEN'S CIVIL WAR LEGACY (VICKSBURG)

McRaven, at 1445 Harrison Street, is thought by many to be the most haunted house in Mississippi. Named after the street name on its original address—McRaven Avenue—it overlooks the confluence of the Yazoo and Mississippi Rivers. The Spanish referred to this high point as Nogales, the Spanish word for "walnuts," eventually giving this area the name Walnut Hills. Before the British officially ceded control of the land south of the Mississippi River to Spain with The Treaty of Paris (1783), the white settlers and their Native American neighbors were in a constant state of war. By the end of the eighteenth century, most of the Spaniards and Indian tribes were gone, leaving the area to wealthy plantation owners. One of these mansions, McRaven, was built in 1798 by Andrew Glass on 408 acres he had claimed along the Mississippi River. Although Glass was reputed to be a notorious highwayman who used his house as hiding place for the booty he had taken from travelers on the Natchez Trace, no historical evidence supports this claim. In fact, Glass was said by those who knew him to be a gentleman who had even served as sheriff. When Glass and his family lived at McRaven, it was nothing more than a two-room cottage with a bedroom above the kitchen. Today, this part of the house is known as the Pioneer Section.

The next part of McRaven was built by Sheriff Stephen Howard, who added the middle dining room and the bedroom above it in the Empire architectural style. Howard and his young wife, Mary Elizabeth Howard, had hoped to turn the house into the focal point of the Mississippi River. Unfortunately, Mary did not live long enough to see their come true. She died in the middle bedroom in late August 1836 after giving birth there.

The large number of deaths that have occurred inside and outside of McRaven seems to account for the high rate of paranormal activity that has been reported here for generations. The earliest report of the haunted side of McRaven dates back to the Civil War. An article appearing in the *Vicksburg Daily Herald* of July 22, 1864, reported that an officer who was spending the night at McRaven as part of the Union army's occupying force was awakened one night by the apparition of a Confederate soldier. Once his eyes were able to focus on the spirit's face in the darkness, he recognized him as the soldier who had served him on board a steamer during the siege of Vicksburg. He could tell that the figure's face was gaunt and mutilated and that his clothing was white. When the officer asked the ghostly intruder his name, he vanished. The article reported that the ghost appeared at night several times afterward in McRaven.

One of the owners of McRaven, John H. Bobb, became part of the collateral damage wrought by the occupying Federal soldiers during General Ulysses S. Grant's siege of Vicksburg. The story goes that on May 14, 1864, Bobb looked out his window at the troops milling around McRaven and

Built by Andrew Glass in 1798, McRaven is haunted by several ghosts, including the spirits of Confederates soldiers who died here when the house served as a field hospital during the Civil War. *Author's collection.*

A chair flipped over during a tour in the Andrew Glass room. *Author's collection.*

was enraged at the sight of several Union soldiers tearing up his beloved gardens. Bobb dashed outside and ordered the men to stop. The Yankees flung curses at the irate homeowner; Bobb retaliated by throwing a brick at them. Later that day, Bobb complained to the Federal officer in command of the occupying troops, General Henry W. Slocum. On his way back home, Bobb was confronted by twenty-five drunken Union soldiers. Recognizing him, the men pulled their guns and fired at Bobb, hitting him twenty-five times. Bobb's widow immediately sold the house and fled to Louisiana.

The ghostly forms of Civil War soldiers have been sighted for years walking around the grounds of McRaven. These apparitions are believed to be the spirits of Confederate soldiers who died while being treated when McRaven served as a field hospital. They were buried in a mass grave in back of the house. A cement marker in the backyard memorializes those soldiers who gave their lives to the Confederate cause.

The interior of McRaven is even more haunted. Former owner Leland French has had several unnerving encounters inside the house. He was walking up the beautiful flying-wing staircase in the entrance to the mansion when he saw a male ghost standing on the landing. He immediately recognized the man's face as that of William Murray from the photographs he had seen. Terror-stricken, French dashed up the stairs and locked himself in the Bobb bedroom. He was so shaken by the incident that, a few days later, French asked an Episcopalian priest to bless the house. On another occasion, French was walking across the floor to answer the telephone when he was pushed down so hard by invisible hands that he hit his face on the floor, and his glasses were pushed into his face. He was cut so severely that he had to have five stitches in his face. An even more painful incident occurred when French was opening a drawer; suddenly, it slammed shut, breaking both of his thumbs. After living at McRaven for over a decade, Leland moved away, as he needed to care for his ailing mother. However, some people believe that it was the violence of his last meeting with one of the ghosts that convinced him to leave.

John H. Bobb is said to be a very strong presence inside the house. His ghost has been seen throughout the house, even joining a tour group on one occasion. In the mid-2010s, the team from the *Ghost Adventures* television show was filming an episode on the first floor when they heard a loud noise in the Bobb bedroom on the second story. They stopped filming and immediately ran upstairs. The men were shocked to find that a red chair and a table with an antique lamp on different sides of the room had somehow been moved across the floor. However, the Gentlemen's Changing Room is the place

Former owner Leland French encountered the ghost of William Murray on the landing of the flying-wing staircase. *Author's collection.*

where Bobb's presence has been sensed by many people. One of the tour guides was walking toward the Gentlemen's Changing Room when she saw a male figure standing perfectly still, staring at her. As the ghost dissipated, she felt as if she had seen the face of the ghost before. Nikki rushed into the parlor, and there, hanging on the wall, was the portrait of the man she had just seen: John H. Bobb.

Many of the disturbances at McRaven resemble the mischievous antics of poltergeists. Tour guides and visitors have reporting hearing doors slamming and alarm clocks going off in the middle of the night. Lights have been known to flicker off and on. One night, one of the tour guides decided to stack up the dominoes in the play area. The next morning, something—or someone—had knocked them all down. In Andrew Glass's bedroom, a tour group was listening to the guide when, all at once, one of the chairs flipped over and fell to the floor. When I visited McRaven on August 31, 2019, the tour guide, Nikki, and I heard a soft thumping sound while standing in the entrance to the parlor. She told me that she has heard random rapping and bumping sounds like this one many times when she and her guests have been alone in the house. Even animals seem to sense that something is not "quite right" about McRaven. While I was touring the house, my wife, Marilyn, and our little Maltese puppy, Holly, were walking up the sidewalk on our way to the house. When we reached the front steps, Holly refused to go any farther. Normally, she bounds up the steps to a strange house when she is walking by my wife's side, but not at McRaven.

The ghosts of several unknown entities have made their presences known inside McRaven as well. The spirit of a teenage girl has appeared on the flying-wing staircase. One tour guide was standing in front of a pile of shrapnel in a little room just outside of Mary Elizabeth Howard's bedroom when he beheld a sight that sent shivers over his body. In front of the door, the figure of a man seemed to be trying to materialize.

The most haunted room in McRaven, according to the tour guides, is Mary Elizabeth Howard's bedroom. Guides have found the impression on a body of the bed when they open up the house in the mornings. A paranormal investigator was using an app on his phone to communicate with the young woman's spirit when the word "baby" appeared on the screen. One of the most significant items in the room is the wedding lace, which is preserved inside a glass picture frame. Years ago, when visitors were able to actually touch the lace, they reported having a very warm feeling course through their fingers.

Not all of the paranormal activity inside McRaven in scary. In fact, some of the ghostly incidents are simply annoying. For example, ever since electric wiring was installed in the old house in 1960, lights sometimes turn themselves on when no one is inside the house. Several times, the local police

Right: John H. Bobb's ghost has been sensed many times in the Gentleman's Changing Room. *Author's collection*.

Below: A paranormal investigator was using his phone app to communicate with the spirit of Mary Elizabeth Howard in her bedroom when the word *baby* appeared on the screen. *Author's collection*.

have responded to reports in the middle of the night that someone has broken into McRaven and turned on the lights. Expecting to find someone stealing the precious antiques, the police are baffled to discover that there is no evidence of forced entry, even though the lights are on.

Despite Leland French's frightening encounter on the flying-wing staircase, he believed that McRaven's ghosts are harmless. McRaven is their home, and they continue to make this point through the disturbances that remind the owners and the docents that they are never really alone in the house.

THE LOST VICTIMS OF THE CHUNKY CREEK TRAIN DISASTER (CHUNKY)

One of the worst train wrecks in U.S. history occurred on February 19, 1863. A train carrying Confederate troops to aid in the defense of Vicksburg against Grant's forces pulled out of Meridian, Mississippi, at 3:00 a.m. The majority of the train's one hundred passengers were soldiers, although a number of civilians were on board as well, including Willis Roy Norman, a Confederate paymaster. Unknown to the engineer of the *Hercules*, debris from severe flooding had lodged against the supports of the bridge across Chunky Creek, thirty-five miles to the west. In an attempt to clear the logs and branches from under the bridge, the section master had accidently caused one of the bridge supports to collapse, severely weakening the structure. To make matters worse, a train had crossed the bridge the day before, forcing the track to shift about six inches out of alignment at the point where it was connected to the bridge.

A lantern hanging from a pole was placed in the middle of the tracks 150 yards from the bridge as a warning to oncoming trains of the damage to the bridge, but it was difficult to see in the darkness. The *Hercules* veered off the track as soon as it entered the bridge, plunging into the icy water below. Approximately seventy-five of the passengers were killed on impact; others were caught up in the swirling water and drowned. Fortunately, the First Battalion of Choctaw Indians was based at a Confederate military training camp nearby. Not long after the train plummeted off the bridge, the Choctaws were pulling passengers out of the water, saving many lives. It took several days to remove all of the bodies and cargo from the creek. Many of the victims were buried along the railroad right-of-way and on Absalom F. Temple's farm.

The Chunky Creek train wreck was covered in newspapers throughout the United States and the Confederacy. Over time, the disaster has been relegated to the status of a historical footnote, except for many of the residents of Chunky. In the 1930s, H.R. Court from Meridian obtained a federal marker for the site, but it was never erected. In late 1984, Jim Dawson from the Lauderdale County Department of Archives and History teamed up with two men from Chunky, Gary "Beetle" Huffmaster and Maxey Baucum, to search for the burial site. They determined that the victims were buried on a small rise above the swampy river bottomland after the discovery of buttons from Confederate uniforms there in the 1940s. A formal survey of the wreck area was conducted by the Newton County Historical and Genealogical Society in 2004. A historical marker was erected at the wreck site in 2005. However, the mass grave of the passengers has never been positively identified.

2

MYSTERIOUS MONSTERS

MISSISSIPPI'S CHUPACABRA
(MENDENHALL AND PICAYUNE)

The Chupacabra, which means "goat sucker" in Spanish, was first sighted in Puerto Rico. It has been variously described as a large animal, the size of a small bear, with spines stretching from the tip of its tail to the top of its head. When Chupacabra-like creatures were reported in northern Mexico and the southwestern United States, most of them were dismissed by authorities as diseased dogs or wolves, with the exception of a strange carcass discovered in Texas by Phylis Canion. DNA tests revealed that the animal was a hybrid of a coyote and a wolf.

Testimony from eyewitnesses indicate that the Chupacabra may have made its way into Mississippi. The first of these sightings was reported by KLTV on October 4, 2011. Truitt Bernard, a resident of Simpson County, said that one afternoon in mid-September, he was walking through an open field near Mendenhall when he saw a creature approximately 130 yards away that he had never seen before. He raised his rifle, sighted the animal through his scope and squeezed the trigger. Scott Barnard, Truitt's son, said, "The animal's back legs were several inches taller than his front legs, his ears were rounded, he had no hair, and his teeth were very long." Scott added that the animal his dad shot was so strange that buzzards would not even circle it. Once word of Truitt Bernard's kill was circulated throughout Simpson County, several locals claimed to have had their own encounters with strange animals in the area.

The next sightings of a Chupacabra-like creature surfaced in 2013. In September, a man told WJTV that he was coon hunting when he found a strange animal in a chicken coop. Thinking that it was a Chupacabra, he shot it and showed the carcass to local animal experts, who informed him that he had killed a mangy dog or coyote. In October, Jennifer Whitfield told a reporter for WLOX that her eleven-year-old son had taken video of a Chupacabra in a lot near their house. Despite the evidence that has been collected in the past few decades, the Chupacabra is still viewed by most zoologists as a creature of myth and legend.

THE MISSISSIPPI WILD MAN
(VICKSBURG AND LOST GAP)

Long before the generic term *Bigfoot* came into general usage in the 1950s, large, hairy, bipedal ape-like creatures have been known by a variety of names in North America. Native Americans living in Washington State referred to them as "Skoocooms." The Sts'ailes people of Canada used the term *Sasquatch*, or *Bigfoot*, for these anthropomorphic beings. In Florida, the crypto-creature is known as the "Skunk Ape." In Louisiana and Mississippi, this animal was called the "Wild Man" in the nineteenth and mid-twentieth centuries.

Stories of the Mississippi Wild Man were first reported in the *Cabira Freeman*, a newspaper in Edensburg, Pennsylvania, in 1867. A band of hunters and their dogs were roaming through the woods near Vicksburg in pursuit of deer. Suddenly, the dogs picked up the scent of their prey and took off through the trees. A large footprint in the mud indicated that the men were chasing something very strange. The track appeared to be human except for the fact that the toes of one foot were turned backward. As the dogs closed in on the animal, the hunters got a close look at their quarry. The newspaper article described it as a being "of about the average height of a man, but of far greater muscular development....It had long hair flowing from it [*sic*] knees, its entire body also seemed to be covered with hair of two to three inches in length, which was a dark brown color. From its upper jaw protruded two very large tusks several inches long." The beast lunged for one of the attacking dogs and buried its tusks in its neck, killing it. The hunters were paralyzed with fear for a few seconds before firing a volley at the monster, which jumped into the river. After what seemed an eternity, the creature rose from the water and screamed. The hunters were all experienced woodsmen who had never heard a sound like this before. The creature sank and rose several times before finally climbing up on the Louisiana side of the river and plunging into the dark woods.

The Mississippi Wild Man surfaced once again in a newspaper article published in California in 1961. In Lost Gap, a rural area five miles east of Meridian, a hairy beast was first sighted by a group of teenagers deep in the woods. One month later, a creature described as a "green-eyed monster that stand six to nine feet tall" was seen running through the countryside "with no pants on and his shirttail flapping in the breeze." For weeks, the police searched the hills and ravines. Toward the end of the hunt, the authorities even used bloodhounds, a helicopter and scores of volunteers, but no trace of the Wild Man was ever found.

No one has definitively uncovered the true of identity of the Mississippi Wild Man. In the nineteenth century, some people assumed that he was a survivor of the New Madrid Earthquake (1811–12) who "turned wild" afterward in the woods. Allen reached a similar conclusion, stating that the "monster" may have been a patient who escaped from a local mental institution. The 1867 sighting differs in that witnesses believed that they encountered a previously unknown species.

TWENTY-FIRST-CENTURY BIGFOOT SIGHTINGS (TISHOMINGO, VICKSBURG AND TOOMSUBA)

Mississippi does not immediately come to mind when one thinks of "Bigfoot Country." However, Donald McDonald, a Bigfoot researcher with the Gulf Coast Bigfoot Research Organization, told a reporter for the *Clarion-Ledger* on September 14, 2014, that he receives between twelve and fifteen reports of Bigfoot sightings in Mississippi every year. The majority of the sightings are unreported because of fear of ridicule. Consequently, only a handful of Bigfoot encounters have received media coverage.

One of the most high-profile of these sightings occurred in Tishomingo on January 5, 2006. A man and his wife were driving home on the Natchez Trace from Florence, Alabama. Around 5:00 p.m., they crossed the state line into Mississippi. After traveling three or four miles, the couple saw what appeared to be a human being jogging along the road about fifty yards from mile marker 307. At the same time, another car was driving toward them in the opposite direction. The couple noticed that the figure was running as fast as a deer. As it crossed over to the left side of the road, the creature tripped and almost fell down. It then continued across the road and melted into the woods.

Because the sighting took place at sunset, the couple was unable to make out any of the beast's facial features. The man described it as being between four and a half and five feet tall. It was clearly running on two legs. He said it was "a little raised" in the back, and it appeared to be a little raised in the front." It was black in color. When the creature tried to catch its balance, the man could tell that its hands and arms were larger than a person's.

The *Clarion-Ledger* published the story of another Bigfoot sighting on September 1, 2014. In November 2013, David Childers was taking photographs of an abandoned playground in the hope of catching paranormal activity. Suddenly, he was distracted by the sound of something large loping through the undergrowth. Before it disappeared, the man could tell that it was approximately six feet tall and that it had "a shaggy coat... like a grayish brown color." Childers believed that the creature was bedding down when he disturbed it with his picture-taking.

A man driving from Toomsuba to his home at 4:30 p.m. saw a large, hairy creature loping across a power-line cut, similar to this one in Lauderdale County. *Author's collection.*

On August 12, Peyton Lassiter was servicing an air-conditioning unit about four hundred yards from the same abandoned playground when he found a nonhuman footprint. Lassiter made a plaster cast of the print and examined it after it hardened. The print measured nine inches in length and was six inches wide at the toes. Embedded in the plaster was a grey hair that matched Childers's description of the creature.

In January 2016, Mississippians who had had Bigfoot encounters were invited to meet in Jackson and share their stories with the cast members and producers of *Finding Bigfoot*, a television show airing on the Animal Planet network. One of these eyewitnesses, Matthew Watson, told an interviewer that, one day, he was driving from work to his home in Toomsuba. At 4:30 p.m., he turned onto a road with a bridge. Watson had just crossed the bridge when he happened to glance over to his left at a power-line cut. Expecting to see deer in the clearing, Watson was shocked to see a very large, hairy beast run across the cut. "Take an Alabama linebacker and grow him by three feet tall, and that's how big it was," Watson said.

McDonald's enthusiasm has been fueled by more than simple curiosity regarding the possibility that a supposedly legendary beast might really exist. While investigating a sighting in the Bienville National Forest one moonlit night, McDonald and his fellow researchers were monitoring their equipment when, all at once, a huge shape loomed in front of them about fifty feet away. McDonald estimated that the creature was seven and a half feet tall. Within the span of just a few seconds, it disappeared into the woods. Because the researchers had ample light and a clear view, they had no doubt that what they caught a brief glimpse of was an actual Bigfoot.

THREE-LEGGED LADY ROAD (COLUMBUS)

Road monsters are a staple of American folklore. For example, a number of people driving along Bray Road in Elkhorn, Wisconsin, have sighted a wolf-like creature on the roadside. In the 1980s, the Lizard Man of Scape Ore Swamp in South Carolina attacked the car of a seventeen-year-old boy while he was changing a tire. In Columbus, Mississippi, Nash Road is said to be the "stomping grounds" of a female phantom known as the "Three-Legged Lady."

The legend of the Three-Legged Lady has been passed down in several variants. In the most commonly told tale, a young girl and her mother lived alone on Nash Road near the lock and dam. One evening, the girl was kidnapped from their home by satanists and dragged screaming into the woods. Once they were out of eyesight of the girl's house, the kidnappers killed her and dismembered her, scattering her body parts throughout the woods. Her distraught mother combed the forest for any trace of the girl but was only able to find one of her legs. Driven mad with grief, the woman sewed her daughter's leg to her own body and continued her search. She can be seen running along Nash Road, looking for the rest of her daughter.

In another variant, a woman's daughter was hit by a car. She was so severely injured that one of her legs was amputated. The poor girl died not long thereafter. Unable to totally relinquish her daughter, her mother sewed the girl's leg to her own body as a kind of remembrance.

Other variants focus on a housewife and infidelity. In the late nineteenth century, a farmer's wife had an affair with a veteran of the Civil War. When her husband discovered the affair, he killed the ex-soldier in a fit of rage and dragged his corpse down Nash Road to a bridge. As he dumped the body over the side, one of the legs was ripped by one of the struts. When the farmer's unfaithful wife discovered her lover's leg, she went insane. The woman brought the leg home and sewed it to her own body. After her husband returned home from the fields, she murdered him and killed herself. Her unquiet spirit still haunts Nash Road.

In still another version, a farmer's wife discovered that he was having an affair with a local woman. The intense love she had for the man turned into anger almost immediately. Once she was convinced that he had fallen asleep, she slipped out of bed and killed him. She then dismembered him, disposing of all of the pieces except for his leg, which she sewed onto her body so that part of him would always be with her. A few days later, the church she and her husband belonged to learned of the murder and informed her that they were going to alert the sheriff. During church services the next day, she locked all of the doors and set fire to the building, incinerating everyone inside. Many people believe that she will kill anyone who threatens to turn her in.

Most of the variants include the rituals one must follow in order to make contact with the Three-Legged Lady. For years, people said that the phantom would appear if one drove up to the church, turned off the car headlights and honked three times. She would then indicate her readiness to race the driver to the end of the road by knocking on the roof of the car. As the Three-Legged Lady raced down the road, she banged into the side of the car. Even though the church is no longer standing, many people still claim to have seen her in the general area.

DEVIL WORSHIPER ROAD (WAYNESBORO)

Stories about a strange creature nicknamed the "Goat Man" can be found in different parts of the country. In Maryland, a scientist who was experimenting with goats in the Beltsville Agricultural Research Center was accidentally infected with a serum that mutated him into a goat-like monster. The Lake Worth Monster in Lake Worth, Texas, is a half-man, half-goat creature with fur and scales that attacked cars in July 1969. The Old Alton Bridge, connecting the cities of Denton and Copper Canyon in Texas, became known as Goatman's Bridge after a black goat farmer was lynched there. His ghost is said to grab and throw rocks at anyone foolhardy enough to cross the bridge. Locals say the Waynesboro-Shubuta Road in Waynesboro is haunted by an entirely different sort of "Goat Man."

The Waynesboro-Shubuta Road in Wayne County is like many other backroads that have acquired a sinister reputation over the years because of stories about satanic cults that performed rituals there. Supposedly, a satanic cult performed its rituals in this out-of-the way place, some of which

A strange creature called the "Goat Man" has been sighted on the Waynesboro Shibuta Road, also known as Devil Worshiper Road. *Author's collection.*

involved human sacrifice. Young people who drive out here to party talk about finding pentagrams spray-painted on old, abandoned buildings by the devil worshipers. These tales are interconnected with a story about a farmer who performed satanic rites on his farm along the Waynesboro-Shubuta Road. The devil tricked the farmer into selling his soul to him in exchange for unlimited power. Instead of granting his wish, the devil transformed the gullible man into a hideous "Goat Man." Standing over seven feet tall, the Goat Man had shaggy white fur all over his body, cloven hooves, glowing eyes and large horns on the top of his head. Some say he wields a pitchfork and has the power to make himself appear and disappear. He became a satyr-like creature, much like the devil himself

Locals have generated a number of spine-tingling tales about their late-night encounters with the Goat Man on Devil Worshiper Road. One eyewitness says he and his friends were forced to stop their car when the Goat Man suddenly appeared in front of them, standing in the middle of the road. While they sat buckled in their seats, trembling, the Goat Man walked around the car, staring at them, before vanishing before their eyes. Another young man said that in 2017, he and a friend were driving around Wayne County one foggy, rainy night when they ended up on Devil Worshiper Road by mistake. When the boys finally found their way back home, they were shocked to discover handprints all over the windshield. Another young man and his brothers had a similar experience two years before. When they reached their home and got out of their car, they found handprints on the hood, roof and doors and a pair of small footprints going up the windshield.

3

MYSTERIES FROM THE SKIES

MISSISSIPPI'S 1977 UFO SIGHTINGS (FLORA)

The Deep South states have a long history of UFO sightings. Many ufologists believe that Louisiana and Mississippi are fertile breeding grounds of the weird and bizarre because of their proximity to large bodies of water. For example, according to Casino.org, the odds of someone in Mississippi having a UFO sighting are 522 to 1. In other words, Mississippi is the thirteenth-most likely state for UFO activity to be witnessed. Between 1940 and 2017, 5,721 UFO sightings have been reported. In fact, one of the most famous UFO encounters in the entire world took place in Flora, Mississippi, in 1977.

On February 10, 1977, a huge airborne object was sighted by approximately two dozen policemen above the tree line in a cotton field just off a country road not far from Flora. A reporter for WAPT, Darren Dedo, asked a deputy to describe what he saw in the sky. To protect the deputy's identity, Dedo referred to him in the interview as "Joe." "It was approximately 15 to 18 feet off the ground, blue in color, kind of metallic blue, portholes around the center of it, shaped like an old spinning top kids used to use." The object floated over the ground for around 45 minutes before zipping off into the sky. National attention focused on an eyewitness account by Deputy Kenneth Creel of the Madison County Sheriff's Department. On the same night, he and Constable James were driving four miles outside of Flora on patrol duty when Creel saw what he thought was a bright star. He realized he was watching something else when the object began increasing in size. Once Creel was able to ascertain that the thing in the sky was disc-shaped, he contacted the Mississippi Highway Patrol. He and his partner stopped the car as soon as the object was about two hundred yards away and turned off the engine so that they could tell whether or not the sounds were being made by the craft. Later, Craft described what he heard as a noise "like a blender…like it was straining, when you first put ice in it." Creel deduced that the object was being piloted when it hovered approximately twenty feet over the police car. Creel gazed upward, hoping to catch a glimpse of the pilot, but all he could make out were "little windows" with "light coming out of them." Creel added that the light changed in color from red to blue to green. The officers watched the UFO for about a minute before Creel turned on the engine and began to back the car up. At the same time, the craft "just picked up and took off" within a few seconds.

Creel, Luke and "Joe" were not the only witnesses to the otherworldly visitor. Just before the object began to speed away, highway patrolman Louis Younger arrived on the scene. He, too, caught sight of the round object floating above the police car. Afterward, Creel and Constable James learned that Deputy Charles Bowering and highway patrolman Joe Chandler had watched the craft from a distance. Police officer Hubert Roberts said that he blinked his police car headlights" at the UFO.

Many UFO researchers consider the Flora case as being one of the most intriguing UFO sightings in the world, because the primary witnesses were officers of the law. Still, some people have called the Flora sighting into question. In a telephone interview with Kenny Creel in 2011, Creel said that he fabricated the story. Joe believes that Creel was pressured by the CIA to change his story. It is possible that other eyewitnesses were also told by the CIA to say nothing about their encounters. Despite Creel's retraction, a number of residents of Flora continue to scan the skies for signs of extraterrestrials. One of these researchers is Pat Frascogna, who was searching through the woods when he found two circular spots about fifteen inches in diameter where no grass would grow. For the most part, though, people seem to be keeping their sightings secret.

THE PASCAGOULA ALIEN ABDUCTION
(PASCAGOULA)

Among the most credible of the people who claim to be alien abductees are Charlie Hickson and Calvin Parker. On October 11, 1973, at 6:00 p.m., forty-two-year-old Hickson and nineteen-year-old Parker, coworkers at a shipyard in Pascagoula, had just gotten off work and were fishing off an abandoned pier just north of where Ingalls Shipyard sits. The sun was going down, but there was a full moon. Suddenly, Parker saw a blue light reflecting off the water. His first thought that the police had arrived and were going to expel them from the area. However, when Parker looked up, he saw two flashing blue lights coming from an oval-shaped craft. "It was hard to tell with the lights so bright, but it looked like it was shaped like a football. I would say, just estimating, [it was] about 80-foot. [It made] very little sound. It was just a hissing noise." Once Parker's eyes adjusted to the glare, he saw three legless creatures float from the craft. Standing about five feet tall, the creatures had gray, wrinkled skin and no discernible necks. Their hands were shaped like the claws of a crab. Each creature had carrot-like growths in place of a nose and ears and a single leg. Hickson said that each creature's legs seemed to be fused together into one leg. He added that they moved stiffly, like robots.

Two of the creatures grabbed Hickson, and one of them grabbed Parker, who believes that he was injected with drugs because he felt immediately relaxed, almost paralyzed. They were then levitated into the spacecraft about one foot above the ground. Hickson said he was examined by a football-shaped device about sixt to eight inches in diameter that scanned his body. Parker was unable to recall what had happened to him aboard the ship until he was placed under hypnotic regression. He said he was taken to a room at the end of a hallway, where he was examined by the most feminine looking of the three creatures. "She took her finger and ran it down my throat and got it behind that thing that hangs down back there and tried to come up in my nasal cavity and that's when it started hurting and I started choking and I got scared and she just kind of telepathically told me, 'Don't be afraid. We aren't going to hurt you.'" Twenty minutes after the examinations began, Hickson and Parker were returned to the bank.

Frightened almost to death, Parker was reluctant to notify the authorities. Hickson, however, insisted that they contact the Jackson County Sheriff's Office. Jackson County captain Glenn Ryder laughed when Hickson told him they had been "picked up" by a UFO, but he told him and Parker to come to the station anyway. In the interrogation room, the sheriff secretly recorded their descriptions of their abduction. Following the interviews, Ryder was convinced that the men were telling the truth. "That boy was especially upset. You can't make up that kind of fear," Ryder said afterward.

Charlie Hickson and Calvin Parker claimed that on October 11, 1973, they were abducted by aliens while fishing off a dock just north of the present site of Ingalls Shipyards. *Wikimedia Commons.*

In the next few weeks, Hickson and Parker were given lie-detector tests, which they passed. The men were questioned under hypnosis by researchers and ufologists, who concluded that Hickson and Parker had suffered severe physical and mental trauma. They were even examined at Keesler Air Force Base in Biloxi for traces of radioactivity and interviewed by military intelligence. Soon, Pascagoula became the center of world attention. Reporters seemed to be everywhere, seeking information about the now-famous abductees. Dr. J. Allen Hynek, formerly with Project Blue Book, interviewed the men and determined that Hickson and Parker were honest men who had had an unnerving experience.

Years later, Hickson said that he had fared better than Parker because he had the benefit of enduring terrifying events during the Korean War. Hickson never changed his story, despite the ridicule that followed him. He appeared on *The Dick Cavett Show* in 1974 and was a featured speaker at various UFO conferences. He published his account of the abduction in *UFO Contact at Pascagoula* (1983). Hickson died on September 9, 2011, at age eighty. Parker chose to avoid public attention until publishing his account of the abduction in his book *The Closest Encounter* (2018).

Hickson and Parker's harrowing experience was verified by other witnesses to the UFO, Jerry and Maria Blair of Theodore, Alabama. In an article published in the *Clarion-Ledger* on March 14, 2019, the couple said that on October 11, 1973, they were sitting in their 1969 Pontiac GTO in the parking lot of Graham's Seafood on the opposite side of the Pascagoula River. They were waiting for a boat captain to take Jerry offshore. Suddenly, Maria noticed a blue light in the sky: "It was just going back and forth. Sometimes, it would just sit there. It went on for 20 to 25 minutes." Initially, she thought she was watching a plane. Then she realized that the light's movement was unlike any aircraft she had ever seen. The strange craft landed 150 to 200 yards from their car. After the craft vanished over the horizon, Jerry and Maria loaded Jerry's gear. While walking down the pier, the couple heard something large splashing in the water. Maria could tell immediately that it was not a dolphin. "I thought it was a person, but now I think it was an alien," Maria said.

Around the same time as Jerry and Maria's sighting, Judy Branning was sitting in a car with her roommate and their dates at a stoplight at Chicot and Highway 90 near the railroad track. Branning and her friends saw some bright lights in the distance that they believed to be the lights of an approaching plane. As the silent craft passed over the car, Branning was able to get a close look. "It was kind of a saucer shape or disc shape with a rounded top. The radio started sounding like it was running through all the stations, and the car went dead. We were freaking out," Branning said. Within a few seconds, the UFO soared upward at a high rate of speed. Branning's close encounter made it difficult for her to sleep that night.

Interest in the Pascagoula Alien Abduction case was revived with the publication of Parker's book in 2018. Pascagoula commemorated the incident by erecting a marker at Lighthouse Park. The commemoration ceremony was held on June 22, 2019.

4

LEGENDARY PLACES

BELLEVUE (PASCAGOULA)

Bellevue is one of the few surviving antebellum homes on Mississippi's Gulf Coast. The three-story Greek Revival home was constructed in 1855 for a New Orleans slave trader named Daniel Graham. Built of native pine and cypress, the house is topped with three dormers and a slate roof. Bellevue's most distinctive architectural feature, however, is its grand self-supported staircase. Over the years, the Grahams acquired a reputation for mistreating their slaves. It was said that Mrs. Graham took a perverse pleasure in beating her slaves to the brink of death. A few of her victims even died of their mistreatment. The bloodstains on the floor of the third story stand as a mute witness to the Grahams' brutality. After the Grahams left the area, their neighbors began spreading rumors about the unquiet spirits of their victims.

At least nine families lived at Bellevue between 1873 and 1902. A few of the owners never really occupied the house. For a short period of time, Bellevue served as a girls' school. The Pollock family bought the house in 1938 and lived there longer than anyone else. Mayor Frank McCanty bought Bellevue from the Pollocks and lived there for three years before selling it to Ingalls Shipbuilding. The corporation completely renovated the old house, turning it into an exclusive club and resort. After several decades, Bellevue was sold to Richard and Diane Scruggs, who restored the home to its nineteenth-century grandeur. Hurricane Katrina damaged the home in

Built in 1855, Bellevue is also known as the Longfellow House because of the mistaken belief that the poet wrote "The Building of a Ship" here. *Author's collection.*

2005; one year later, it was purchased by Dr. Tracy and Randy Roth, who repaired the damage and made Bellevue their private residence.

The various owners of Bellevue have given rise to a number of different legends. One of the tales concerns the origin of the house, nicknamed the "Longfellow House." Local residents say that the beloved American poet Henry Wadsworth Longfellow visited Bellevue for a short while in the late nineteenth century. During his stay, he is said to have written a poem, "The Building of a Ship," about the construction of a ship in Pascagoula Bay. However, a professor at Spring Hill College named Alice Hill Lauchaussee insists that the story is a myth, inspired primarily from Longfellow's references to the timbers "from Pascagoula's sunny bay" in the poem. She found no evidence indicating that Longfellow had ever traveled farther south than Virginia.

The ghost stories told about Bellevue have their source in the antebellum era. According to legend, one of the Grahams' slaves was beaten severely and dragged out to the woods to die. He is said to be an angry spirit who walks back and forth in the upstairs rooms. He was also credited with slapping

Bobbie Slaughter, the night manager of the hotel. She claimed that the slap was so loud that other people heard it. Slaughter also reported hearing a juke box come on at 3:00 a.m. It continued playing until 5:00 a.m. "We would hear babies crying, toilets flushing, café doors opening and closing," Slaughter said. "Sometimes, it would sound like a party going on upstairs. You'd hear conversations and ice clinking in glasses, but when you got upstairs, the noise stopped." Over time, the paranormal activity escalated. After glasses started shattering at the bar, the hotel staff contacted psychics, who determined that Bellevue was haunted either by three ghosts or by a single ghost going through three stages of life.

A number of the occupants of Bellevue have had eerie encounters in the house as well. Some of these disturbances include hearing doors slam and seeing objects levitate and fly across the room. The past, it seems, is still alive and well at Bellevue.

THE LYRIC THEATRE (TUPELO)

In 1912, a businessman named R.F. Goodlett secured financing for the construction of a vaudeville theater called the Comus. In 1931, the M.A. Lightman Company chain purchased the building and converted it into a movie theater. The company immediately set about making a number of changes to the building, including the addition of its art deco exterior and its trademark marque. In 1936, the Lyric Theatre gained notoriety as one of the largest buildings to survive an F5 tornado that raged through Tupelo on April 5, 1936. With wind speeds up to three hundred miles per hour and a funnel cloud three city blocks wide, the tornado was so strong that flying pine needles penetrated the trunks of trees. The official number of deaths is 233, not including an unrecorded number of African Americans who lost their lives. A field hospital was set up inside the Tupelo Theatre, where an untold number of injured and dying residents were treated by doctors who sterilized their surgical instruments in the theater's popcorn poppers. The building's crawl space was used as a makeshift morgue for the victims who died inside the theater. The Tupelo tornado of 1936 is ranked as the fourth-deadliest twister in the history of the United States. The Lyric Theatre continued showing movies until 1984. It stood abandoned for several years and barely escaped demolition when it was bought by the Tupelo Community Theatre.

The tornado of 1936 is long gone, but at least one of its victims has taken up residence inside the historic theater. The most active presence has been christened "Antoine" by the theater's employees. He is said to be the spirit of a child who was injured and died as he was being treated inside the theater or who died outside of the theater. Many of the unexplained occurrences inside the theater are credited to Antoine's mischievous spirit, especially during its big Halloween fundraiser, "The Haunted Theatre." Bobby Geno, who has served as director for a number of plays at the Lyric Theatre, said that something really strange happened while he was removing large sheets of plastic from the stage one night after the Haunted Theatre closed. He turned his back for a minute; when he turned back around, Geno was surprised to find that only one sheet of plastic remained on the stage. He believed that this was Antoine's way of expressing his displeasure with the way Geno was cleaning the stage. Tracie Conwell, the director of the Haunted Theatre, was inside the building alone during the fundraiser when, suddenly, all the lights went out. Speaking to Antoine, Conlin said, "Antoine, I've never messed with you. Don't mess with me!" Almost instantly, the lights came back on.

The Lyric Theatre, built in 1912, doubled as a field hospital and a morgue following the tornado that ravaged Tupelo on April 15, 1936. *Author's collection.*

Paranormal activity has been reported inside the theater at other times of the year as well. Tom Booth, the executive director of the Tupelo Community Theatre, credited giggling and other strange noises to the childish spirit. In an interview with the *Daily Journal*, he distinctly recalled hearing childish laughter when he returned to the theater one night to pick up some flowers. Thinking that a volunteer was trying to frighten him, Booth yelled out, "Ha Ha! Very funny!" However, shivers ran up his spine when no one replied. Booth believes he had another encounter with Antoine when the keys he thought he had lost suddenly turned up in a Plexiglass container on his desk.

Other bizarre events have occurred at the Lyric Theatre that do not seem to be the work of a playful ghost. Some people claim to have seen a spectral green light bobbing through the theater. One day, Booth was sitting at his desk when he was startled by what sounded like a collapsing wall. He realized that the sound he had heard was unearthly when a search of the theater produced nothing. Despite the high number of unexplained occurrences, Booth does not feel that the ghost or ghosts that haunt the Lyric Theatre mean any harm. Speaking of the unnerving incidents that happen with some regularity inside the old theater, Booth admits, "There's just some things you can't identify."

THE CHAPEL OF THE CROSS (MANNSDALE)

In 1819, John T. Johnstone moved from North Carolina to Madison County, Mississippi, where he established Annandale Plantation. Johnstone had planned to build a chapel on his planation, but he died in 1848 before his dream could become a reality. Determined to build her husband's church, Margaret most likely hired Frank Wills to design the Chapel of the Cross in 1850. Construction of the chapel was completed in 1852. Shortly thereafter, Margaret deeded the church and the property to the Episcopal Diocese of Mississippi. A few years later, after work on the chapel was finished, Margaret built an Italian Renaissance mansion for her and her family that she called Annandale. In 1924, Annandale burned to the ground. The chapel fell into disuse after the Civil War and was in dire need of repair when Margaret Johnstone's granddaughter persuaded the diocese to reactivate the congregation. In 1956, the Chapel of the Cross was restored. Today, the Chapel of the Cross is a thriving Episcopalian church. It is famous for not only its architecture and graveyard but also its romantic ghost story.

People passing by the Chapel of the Cross at night have heard the deep, sonorous tones of an organ. *Author's collection.*

The tale begins in 1855, when Henry Vick's carriage broke down just outside of the Johnstone plantation. Vick was a member of the congregation of Reverend Newitt Vick, who founded Vicksburg. He was smitten with the beauty of sixteen-year-old Helen, and the two soon fell in love. They became engaged two years later, but Margaret convinced the couple to delay their marriage until Helen turned twenty. In accordance with her mother's wishes, Helen set the date for her wedding on May 21, 1859, her birthday. However, four days later, her fiancé was shot and killed in a duel in Mobile. His body was delivered to Annandale while Helen was finalizing plans for her wedding. The heartbroken girl accompanied her beloved to the family plot in the graveyard behind the chapel on the day that was supposed to have been the happiest of her life. She eventually recovered from the tragedy and married an Episcopal priest named George Harris in 1862. In 1896, the couple moved to Rolling Fork and built a house, Mount Helena, where they raised three children. George died in 1911, and Helen followed him in death six years later. People who knew her say she had never totally recovered from the death of her first love.

The ghost of Helen Johnstone has been seen weeping at the grave of her fiancé, Henry Vick, who was killed in a duel in Mobile, Alabama. *Author's collection.*

A number of ghost stories have attached themselves to the Chapel of the Cross. Many people claim to have seen the ghost of a twenty-year-old girl kneeling by the grave of Henry Vick. The ghosts of two children have been sighted climbing up a tree in the graveyard and perching on one of the branches. A number of other ghosts are said to stroll in and out of the graveyard periodically. The interior of the chapel is reputed to be haunted as well. Bloodstains on the chapel floor have resisted all attempts to remove them. The deep, sonorous sound of the organ has been heard by passersby late at night.

MISSISSIPPI'S PREHISTORIC "GREAT WALL" (CLAIBORNE COUNTY)

On November 7, 1900, the *New York Times* published an article titled "Mississippi's Great Wall: A Mysterious Structure Whose Builder No One Knows." The article focuses on a prehistoric wall that was said to begin at

Raymond, Mississippi, and wind through Copiah County overlooking the valley of Brandywine Creek. The author of the article based his story on information provided by Thomas Watson of Hazlehurst. Watson had sent Governor Andrew Logino a pencil drawing of a pile of stones in Claiborne County that he believed could be used to build a new state capitol. Watson said that the whitish or grayish white stones measured from six to eight feet in length and three feet wide by two feet thick. The weight of the stones varied from two to three tons. According to Watson, local contractors had already removed a portion of the wall, up to a width of eight blocks, to use on their building projects. The stones had been sealed together with cement, making it difficult to separate the blocks. Describing the appearance of the wall, the author of the article wrote, "The seams between the tiers are perfectly straight, and each block of stone is perfectly horizontal in position, and these blocks are smoothly dressed on the edges and ends, while the broad surfaces are rough, showing a broken surface brought down to a level plane, but not dressed." Watson believed that cave-ins near the wall pointed to the possibility that large caves and maybe even underground cities would be found some day.

Inspired by the story in the *New York Times*, David Ives Bushenell of Clarksdale, Mississippi, traveled to Brandywine in 1901 to determine for himself whether or not a prehistoric race had built a massive wall in Claiborne County. Three years later, Bushnell published his findings in a book titled *Mississippi River Valley*. He determined that the wall-like structure described by Watson was nothing more than a perpendicular stratum of white sandstone that had been created by natural forces. The "blocks" had been formed by what he called "natural cleavage." The "cement" holding the blocks together was decomposed limestone.

In 2011, Walt Grayson, a storyteller and broadcaster for television station WLBT in Jackson, Mississippi, resurrected the story of the Brandywine Wall. Grayson had received word that two residents of Copiah County, Stacey Saucier and his brother, were walking through a section of hunting land they had just acquired when they discovered a large outcropping of limestone. The men estimated that the "structure" ran about seventy-five yards along the creek. He traveled to Brandywine and was disappointed to find that nothing remained of the community but the old Brandywine Methodist Church. While he was driving around the area, Grayson noticed a yard full of rocks. The owner of the property, Jeff Leonard, told him that there was a large deposit of rocks behind his house. Grayson concluded that beds of rock like this one might resemble a wall if the layer of soil on top had been removed. As far as he was concerned, the Brandywine Wall was entirely natural.

THE MYSTERIES OF DEER ISLAND (BILOXI)

Just offshore from Ocean Springs and Biloxi, Deer Island is a Mississippi Coastal Preserve. It is home to nine endangered species, including the great blue heron. However, human beings have also lived on the island for centuries. Long before the birth of Christ, Native Americans hunted and fished here. By the eighteenth century, the French had occupied Deer Island. In the early twentieth century, it was a tourist destination for families eager to spend time at the amusement park. Nature reclaimed Deer Island following the mass destruction caused by Hurricane Camille in 1969. Today, the only evidence of a human presence on the island is its ghost stories.

One of Deer Island's ghosts first appeared in the *Sun Herald* newspaper on May 20, 1922. According to the writer Anthony Ragusin, two fishermen who had been fishing after dark decided to camp out on Deer Island. While they were making coffee, the men heard something rustling in the palmetto bushes. Thinking that wild hogs were digging around in the sand, the men ignored the noises and continued building their fire. After a while, the ruckus aroused the men's curiosity, and they decided to investigate. They had just

In the early 1920s, a couple of fishermen were terrified by the sight of a headless skeleton on Deer Island, where a pirate captain was said to have buried his treasure. *Wikipedia.*

taken a few steps into the palmettos before they came to an abrupt halt. They were horrified to see a headless skeleton standing in the center of the palmettos. Fueled by fear, the fishermen ran to the boat at full speed with the phantom in full pursuit. The men had barely shoved off before their pursuer was close enough to grab them.

Ragusin's source for this hair-raising tale was Captain Eugen Tibler Sr., whose family had deep roots in Biloxi as businessmen, oystermen and fishermen. He was renowned as a walking repository of Gulf Coast history and lore. Ragusin, who had related many legends in his newspaper column, "Back with Father Time in the Early Days of the Mississippi Coast," pointed out the similarities between Tibler's story and a much older yarn concerning a pirate ship that landed on Deer Island in the early nineteenth century. The captain chose the isolated piece of land as the ideal place to bury the crew's booty. After the ship's ill-gotten gains had been safely deposited under the sand, the captain singled out one of the most robust of the pirates for a "special honor." While the young man was standing in front of the captain, one of his lieutenants sneaked behind him, drew his cutlass and decapitated him. The crew buried their hapless shipmate so that his restless spirit would stand guard over the treasure for eternity. At the end of the article, Ragusin said that the ghastly specter had appeared to other people over the years as well. One of these eyewitnesses was a fisherman from Biloxi who was walking through Deer Island with two of his friends when, suddenly, a headless skeleton emerged from the palmettos. All three men bolted from the horrible figure and hurried back to their boat.

Ragusin also wrote about a ghost light that has been sighted on the island for years. Captain Tibler told him that in 1891, he and his brother were rowing in Back Bay at 2:00 a.m. when a bluish light appeared about a foot over the surface of the water and flitted off in the direction of Ocean Springs. Ragusin believed that this sighting is probably connected somehow to the legend of the "Firewater Ghost," a spectral sentry that carries a lantern as he makes his rounds across the island. No recent sightings have been reported. The possibility also exists that this legend is a variant of the tale of the headless skeleton.

STUCKEY'S BRIDGE (CHUNKY)

In 1847, Lauderdale County issued a contract for the construction of a wooden bridge across the Chunky River near Chunky, Mississippi.

Construction of the bridge was completed three years later. In 1901, the Virginia Bridge and Iron Company replaced the older bridge with a new iron bridge. In 1984, Stuckey's Bridge was designated a Mississippi Landmark. On November 16, 1988, it was added to the National Register of Historic Places. Stuckey's Bridge also holds the unofficial title as one of the most haunted bridges in the entire state.

According to legend, Stuckey was an outlaw who was left behind in Lauderdale County by the Dalton Gang in the first half of the nineteenth century. He soon realized that an enterprising criminal—like himself—could make some money off people floating down the Chunky River. He built an inn on the riverbank in the hope of attracting flatboat men on their way to sell their goods in Meridian. After the first bridge was built, he walked across it at night, swinging a lantern as a signal to travelers on the river looking for a place to spend the night. As soon as they went to sleep, Stuckey crept into their bedroom and clubbed them to death. He then collected their possessions and buried their bodies along the riverbank. Locals say that as many as twenty of his victims were hastily interred in shallow graves. Stuckey is said to have dumped a number of corpses into the Chunky River as well. Eventually, word of Stuckey's nefarious activities reached the authorities, who tried him and hanged him from the railings of the bridge outside of his inn. After he stopped "kicking," the sheriff cut the rope. Witnesses to the execution took a great deal of satisfaction in watching Stuckey's body fall into the same river that was the final resting place for so many innocent people.

However, Stuckey's story does not end here. For over a century, people have claimed to see an elderly man walk across the bridge, lantern in hand. Some passersby claim to have seen Stuckey's body dangling from the bridge. A number of people swear that they heard a loud splashing sound while they were walking across the bridge. When they peered over the railing, they beheld an eerie glow emanating from the spot where Stuckey's body plunged into the water. By the twenty-first century, many of the ghost stories about Stuckey's Bridge were told by young people looking for an out-of-the-way place to party and prove their courage. One resident of Meridian said that he and his girlfriend were floating down the Chunky River with four other couples when they decided to row ashore at Stuckey's Bridge and tell ghost stories. They were sitting down along the riverbank when they heard someone walking across the bridge. They ran toward the sound and were shocked to find that no one was there. In 2005, a young man and his best friend drove their car over the bridge. The young men pulled over at the end

In the mid-nineteenth century, a murderous outlaw named Stuckey was hanged from this bridge for killing and robbing guests at his inn along the Chunky River. *Wikimedia Commons.*

of the bridge and started to walk across it. As they looked over the railing, they were surprised to see a swinging light out in the river. Without warning, the strange ball of light flew out of the river and passed straight through them. The young men immediately rushed over to their car and drove off as fast as they could.

Stuckey's Bridge was closed in 2011. That fact has not deterred the hundreds of thrill-seekers who walk across the old bridge in the hope of encountering Stuckey's ghost. The inability of historians to find any mention of a member of the Dalton Gang named Stuckey does not seem to matter, either. After all, when have southerners ever allowed the absence of historical verification interfere with their enjoyment of a good legend?

THE CAUSEYVILLE GENERAL STORE (CAUSEYVILLE)

The Causeyville General Store is one of a cluster of three historic buildings. R.G. Reynolds built the original structures—the gristmill and the mill store—

in 1860. For over thirty years, settlers and Choctaw Indians purchased a variety of sundries in the mill store, including groceries, hardware, medicine and turpentine. When T.J. Bostick built the general store in 1895, the mill store was converted into a cotton warehouse. Joseph Grantham purchased the store in 1910. Around this time, Bostick added walls in the back of the store to enclose the family residence. Grantham's clientele were, for the most part, farmers, who often bartered for goods at the store with eggs, vegetables and poultry. In the 1920s, the general store adapted to the needs of the growing community with the addition of a soda fountain, a post office and a doctor's office. Like many country doctors as the time, Dr. William Anderson traveled around the countryside making house calls. In 1942, the Grantham family sold the general store, the gristmill and the mill store to Everett W. Hagwood. Over the years, a number of different members of the Hagwood family have owned the property. Joanne Hagwood Irby and her husband purchased the store from her father, Leslie Hagwood Sr. In the 1980s, Joanne's brother Leslie bought the store. Leslie and his wife, Dorothy, then undertook the process of restoring the buildings. The Causeyville General Store and gristmill were added to the National Register of Historic Places in 1986. Dorothy Hagwood took over the store following her husband's death

The Causeyville General Store is protected by the ghost of a black dog named Babe, who is buried near the store. *Author's collection.*

in 1995. Today, the old store is filled with memorabilia from yesteryear. Lingering among the antique signs and World War II posters are, some people say, the spirits of the past.

Many of the tales told about the Causeyville General Store originated with the employees. In her book *Country Stores of Mississippi*, author June Davison includes stories told by former store clerk Caroline Smith, who recalled hearing snoring coming from the back room where T.J. Bostick took his afternoon naps. She also said that cans that had been stacked up during the day would be scattered all over the floor the next morning. She also heard disembodied footsteps when she was all by herself in the store. Another employee named Bob said that he heard a piano playing in the backroom. Balls of light have been sighted flying through the store for many years.

Lured by the tales of supposedly supernatural phenomena, a local group of "ghost hunters" named "Orbservations" conducted an all-night investigation of the Causeyville General Store in February 2006. Not only did the group verify the reports of orbs in the old store, but their cameras also captured a cloud of dust hovering over the pianos. One of the most significant pieces of evidence collected that night was the soft sound of a player piano that played most of the night. The members also recorded a sneezing sound in the back room where one of the owners died. It turned out that the "sneezing ghost" was the first ghost story Dorothy Hagwood had heard about the place.

In an interview with *Meridian Star* reporter Jennifer Jacobs in 2011, Dorothy Hagwood discussed the other types of paranormal activity that she had experienced over the years. Electronic devices, like a toy train, tend to turn off and on by themselves. Cans fly off the shelves if they have been stacked incorrectly. Dorothy heard someone in high heels walking on the wooden floors when she was all alone. This eerie sound is usually accompanied by the scent of lavender perfume. Traces of cherry tobacco occasionally waft through the store as well. Dorothy insists, though, that the most frightening object in the entire store is an old lamp suspended from the ceiling. She explained why the lamp is tied to a large flat iron: "Out of the clear blue, you'll look up, and that thing is going as far as the chain will let it, round and round and round…I got afraid it was going to break loose, so I tied it down." One of her employees actually quit because the lamp was spinning around while she was in the store by herself.

One of the store's ghosts, however, is a comforting presence. Shortly after Dorothy Hagwood took over operation of the store in the late 1990s, a stray dog showed up. Taking pity on the animal, she began feeding him. Soon, the dog she named "Babe" began greeting customers on the front porch. She also turned out to be good judge of character. One day, Babe started growling at a group of men who were acting strangely inside the store. Afterward, the sheriff told Dorothy that her description of the men matched that of a band of robbers who had been holding up businesses in the area. Dorothy was so attached to Babe that she buried him near his home after he died of bone cancer. One day not long after Babe died, a lady walked into the store and asked Dorothy where the black dog with the white chest was. She expected to find the dog sitting on the porch, because she and her children had seen him there a few days earlier when she came by the store. The woman was shocked when Dorothy informed her that the dog she had described had died. Dorothy Hagwood admits that the dog the woman saw was probably a look-alike that had taken up Babe's spot on the porch, but she takes comfort in the possibility that her beloved dog could still be a protective presence in her life.

ROWAN OAK (OXFORD)

Colonel Robert Shegog moved to Oxford in 1844. Four years later, he completed the construction of his family home in the primitive Greek Revival style. The studs used in the house were hand-hewn. The house sits on four acres of land, surrounded by twenty-nine acres of forest called Bailey's Woods. The long drive to the house is lined with an "alley" of cedars. Renowned author William Faulkner purchased the house and grounds in the 1930s. He renamed the "Old Bailey Place," as it was known at the time, "Rowan Oak" after a mythical tree that was believed to have the power to ward off evil spirits. Faulkner immediately set about restoring the house after buying it. The renovation process continued in the 1950s. In 1972, Faulkner's daughter, Jill Faulkner Summers, sold the house to the University of Mississippi. Rowan Oak was renovated once again in the early 2000s, this time with the financial assistance of Ole Miss law school graduate John Grisham. The first curator, Bev Smith, was followed by novelists Howard Bahr and Cynthia Shearer and the most recent curator, William Griffith.

For many years, curators and tour guides have shared the story of Rowan Oak's haunted past with tourists. The best-known tales were told by Faulkner himself. Dr. Leighton Pettis, a childhood friend of Jill Faulkner's, recalled her

Author William
Faulkner fabricated
a story about
Judith Shegog,
who jumped from
the second-story
balcony following
the death of her
lover. *flickr.com*.

father telling stories on Halloween night about Colonel Shegog's daughter, Judith, who died in the house in 1864. Curator William Griffith said that the story exists in several variants because Faulkner changed important plot details every time he told it. In one version, Judith jumps from the second-story balcony after her lover is killed by another soldier. According to the most popular version, Judith kills herself after learning that her lover, Michael Johnson of the Southern Illinois Volunteers, died on the battlefield. All of the variants end with Judith's broken body being interred under the old magnolia tree. Faulkner finished the tale by stating that every year on the anniversary of her death, Judith's restless spirit walked down the staircase from the second floor, passed through the front door and made her way across the lawn to her grave. He then asked for someone to take a lighted candle and walk over to the tree where she was supposed to have been buried. "One of us would volunteer, and either we would shake so bad from walking down there or the wind would get it, but the candle would always blow out. We all thought Judith blew it out, and we'd all run in the house screaming." In his book *Faulkner: A Biography*, Joseph Blotner tells the story of one Halloween party in particular when Faulkner frightened his guests with a rattling chain and a white sheet fluttering in the wind.

As convincing as Faulkner's "production" of the tale was for his listeners, the fact is that the story is a complete fabrication. In fact, the Shegogs did not have a daughter named Judith. "The house needed a ghost. That's the inspiration behind the Judith tale from Faulkner," Griffith said. Although he has had no personal encounters with the supernatural in the house, Griffith is not 100 percent certain that Rowan Oak is "ghost free." In 2000, one year after he was hired as curator, Griffith prepared for the renovation of Rowan

Oak by photographing the furniture in its original positions so that he and his staff would know where to place each piece after the workmen had left. Two years later, Griffin examined the photographs taken of the area in back of the house from Faulkner's wife's bedroom on the second floor and discovered something unsettling. In one photograph, two people are sitting on a bench in front of the arbor and servants' quarters. However, nothing can be seen behind the two figures. It is as if something is blocking the view of the arbor and servants' quarters. "There's this dark void encroaching around the figures," Griffith said.

Two other employees, Amanda Malloy and Sara Altenhoff, have had strange experiences inside Rowan Oak as well. One morning, Altenhoff opened the house and walked into Faulkner's bedroom. Lying on the bed was a pillow that appeared to have the indentation of a head on it. Chills ran up her spine when she realized that someone must have been lying on the bed during the night. Malloy has heard the jiggling of doorknobs within the house when she was all by herself. It sounds as if someone is trying to enter the rooms. Visitors and staff have reported seeing Faulkner's ghost prowling around the house at night, seemingly on the lookout for intruders. It is no wonder that many employees at Rowan Oak are reluctant to stay there after the sun goes down.

THE DEVIL'S PUNCHBOWL (NATCHEZ)

Not far from the Natchez City Cemetery is the Devil's Punchbowl, a huge, semicircular natural cut in the bluff along the Mississippi River. It is almost completely overgrown with kudzu vines. At the very bottom is a pool of water. No scientific explanation has fully explained its existence, lending an aura of mystery to the entire area. This geological anomaly has fueled the imagination of people living and traveling around the Natchez Trace. The violent nature of many of these tales suggests that the Devil's Punchbowl is aptly named.

For generations, people have shared tales of buried treasure and river pirates. Land pirates like John Murrel and the Harpe brothers were said to have disposed of the bodies of people they robbed and murdered on the Natchez Trace for years in the Devil's Punchbowl. Supposedly, these brigands even bet each other which corpse hit the bottom first.

One of the most legendary of these murderers and robbers was Joseph Thompson Hare. His base of operations was New Orleans, but his criminal activity extended throughout the Natchez Trace and as far north as Kentucky. Hare dressed like a dandy and, to all appearances, was a gentleman. However, Joseph Hare was actually a brutal, heartless man who is reputed to have murdered as many as one hundred people. One of his victims was his mistress. When Hare discovered that she was unfaithful, he ordered his cronies to bury her alive somewhere in the Devil's Punchbowl, wearing only the jewels he had given her. For years, her ghost has offered gold and jewels to anyone who will relocate her body to hallowed ground. Her apparition has also been sighted along the Natchez Trace with Hare's laughing spirit.

Unlike many of the criminals who preyed on travelers on the Natchez Trace, Hare was a literate man who kept a journal. In one of his entries, Hare reported seeing a beautiful white horse across the road. He walked within six feet of the horse before the animal vanished. Hare interpreted this vision as a sign sent from God to make him repent. He never did. Joseph Thompson Hare was hanged in Baltimore, Maryland, on September 10, 1818.

One of the most tragic stories to have grown up around the Devil's Punchbowl concerns the fate of ten thousand slaves who were freed during the Union occupation of Natchez in July 1863. According to Don Estes, former director of the Natchez City Cemetery, "[The Union Army] decided to build an encampment for them at Devil's Punchbowl, which they walled off." As many as seventy-five people are reputed to have died every day as the result of bad food, tainted water and diseases like smallpox. They were buried in shallow graves inside the Devil's Punchbowl. Historical proof of the interment of the freed slaves is difficult to find. However, the bones that have been washing out of the Devil's Punchbowl for years stand as mute evidence of crimes that have taken place there. To this day, many local residents of Natchez refuse to eat the wild peaches that grow there for fear of what has been fertilizing the soil.

THE BILOXI LIGHTHOUSE (BILOXI)

In 1847, the Biloxi Lighthouse was built by the Murray and Hazlehurst Foundry for $6,347. The iron lighthouse was forty-seven feet tall and was equipped with nine lamps. The first lighthouse keeper, Marcellus J. Howard, was replaced on April 11, 1854, by a single mother named Mary Reynolds. She distinguished herself in 1863 by keeping the light burning during a hurricane. During the Civil War, the lighthouse was put out of commission. In November 1866, the lighthouse was reactivated. The new keeper, Perry

According to legend, the Biloxi Light was painted black in 1866 as a sign of mourning for President Abraham Lincoln, who was assassinated the year before. *Author's collection.*

Younghans, was not on the job for very long before he became ill. Unable to carry out his duties, Perry was replaced by his wife, Maria Younghans, on December 6, 1867. On October 21, 1893, Maria displayed the same sort of pluck as her predecessor, Mary Reynolds, by keeping the light burning during a hurricane. After retiring on December 31, 1918, she was replaced by her daughter Miranda, who held the position of lighthouse keeper until 1929. The lighthouse achieved fame in 1960 as the site of a "wade-in," during which protestors expressed their objection to segregation. The Biloxi Lighthouse survived the ravages of Hurricane Camille in 1969, but the lighthouse keeper's home was completely destroyed. The lighthouse itself suffered extensive damage during Hurricane Katrina. Restoration of the historic structure was completed in 2010.

The lighthouse's signature legend was generated after it reopened in 1866. It was covered with a coat of black coal tar to prevent its iron skin from rusting. However, many locals believed the lighthouse was painted black as a sign of mourning following the assassination of President Abraham Lincoln. Edmond Boudreaux Jr., author of *Legends and Lore of Mississippi Golden Gulf Coast*, believes that in 1866, President Lincoln would not have been mourned by most of the residents of the Deep South because, at the time, he was still considered to be the enemy. This is a good example of a legend that has sprung up because of mistaken assumptions based on inadequate information.

THE WITCH DANCE (TUPELO)

Tales of barren patches of ground have been staples of southern folklore for centuries. For example, the Devil's Tramping Ground, a forty-foot circle of bare ground in a camping spot near the Harper's Crossroads area in Bear Creek, North Carolina, is reputed to be the place where the devil walks around at night as he plans his strategy for snaring more souls. In Bath, North Carolina, a series of bare spots have become the subject of a legend known as the "Devil's Hoof Prints," which commemorates the ill-fated horse race between a foolhardy gambler and the devil. A similar spot where grass does not grow can be found at milepost 233.2 on the Natchez Trace. A sign erected by the National Park Service has labeled this botanical anomaly the "Witch Dance."

In the late eighteenth and early nineteenth centuries, witches from miles around began congregating in the mound area to conduct their nightly ceremonies, which involved feasting and dancing. It was said that grass would not grow in the places where their bare feet touched the ground. Convinced that these patches of ground had become tainted, the Choctaw and Chickasaw Indians avoided them entirely. The negativity attached to the Witch Dance became even more pronounced when an outlaw and murderer named Micajah "Big" Harpe was shown the bare spots by an Indian guide while prowling the Natchez Trace for victims. When the guide told Big Harpe the stories about the witches' wicked rites, he showed his disdain for the Indian's superstitious nature by jumping from one bare spot to the next. Not long thereafter, a posse captured Big Harpe in Kentucky. One of the members, a man whose wife and baby had been killed by Big Harpe and his brother, Little Harpe, cut off his head and placed it in a tree. Several months later, a witch ground Big Harpe's skull into powder, which she used to cure her son of epilepsy.

A supernatural aura still envelops the Witch Dance. Some people claim to have heard the beating of tom-toms during the night. The cackling of the witches is carried on the wind, usually at midnight, through the hills and

People passing by at night have heard the beating of tom-toms and the cackling of witches at Witch Dance. *Wikimedia Commons*.

hollows. Spectral Indians have been sighted riding their skeletal horses over the Witch Dance. Ghost lights dance through the woods. Unearthly screams pierce the nighttime silence, usually around midnight. Some witnesses claim to have seen phantom forms clothed in white or in phosphorescent robes. The fact that much of the barren earth has been covered by kudzu has not diminished the power that the strange area has over the imagination. Not surprisingly, few people venture into the Witch Dance after sundown.

KING'S TAVERN (NATCHEZ)

King's Tavern, the oldest structure in Natchez, was built in 1769 as a blockhouse for Fort Panmure. The wood used in construction of the building was taken from old sailing ships that had been sold for scrap and from flatboats dismantled in Natchez because they could not be taken back up the river. Sun-dried bricks were also used in construction of the building. Following the Revolutionary War, the fort was no longer needed, so, in 1789, it was purchased by Richard King for use as a tavern, a "post office" where packages could be picked up and delivered and as a private residence for himself and his family on the third floor. Because Natchez is situated on the terminus of the Natchez Trace, King's Tavern did a thriving business with weary travelers and the outlaws who preyed on them. Some of the tavern's most notorious customers from this period were the Harpe brothers, who stayed at the inn on several occasions. Business fell off after a new era of travel on American rivers was ushered in by Robert Fulton's steamboat the *Clermont* in 1807. King sold the tavern in 1817 to Henry Postlewaith. Following his death from yellow fever on August 27, 1823, his wife, Elizabeth, and her eight children moved into the tavern and converted it into a private residence. Members of the Postlewaith family continued living in the old house for 147 years. In 1970, the Pilgrimage Garden Club of Natchez purchased the building and reverted it into a restaurant called the Post House Restaurant. Yvonne Scott bought the restaurant in 1987 and opened it as King's Tavern. In 2005, Tom Drinkwater and Shawyn Mars purchased the property from Yvonne Scott.

Most of the ghost stories and legends were generated in the period when the old tavern was owned by the Garden Club and Yvonne Scott. The most familiar legend connected to King's Tavern concerns a sixteen-year-old server remembered only as "Madeleine" who eventually gave in to Richard King's advances, even though she was engaged to someone else at the time. After Mrs. King learned of her husband's infidelity, Madeleine disappeared. Of course, rumors spread throughout Natchez that King's wife was involved somehow, but she was never brought to trial. In the minds of many residents of Natchez, the mystery was solved in 1932, when a sewage line was being installed in the historic building. One day, the workers dug up something much more gruesome than dirty. Lying in a shallow grave were the skeletons of two men and a woman, as well as a Spanish dagger. The discovery led to speculation that Mrs. King had hired two men to murder her rival in love and then murdered them as well, concealing the evidence of her crime inside the tavern. The skeletons were reburied in the potter's field of the Natchez City cemetery. Like many legends, this one does hold up to close scrutiny. Mike Chapman, team leader of NAPS (Natchez Area Paranormal Society), said that after conducting extensive research, he was unable to find any evidence that three bodies were actually uncovered inside King's Tavern, although a dagger was found there during renovations. In addition, no proof has ever been produced of Mrs. King's involvement in Madeleine's disappearance.

Richard King operated what came to be known as King's Tavern from 1789 to 1817. *flickr.com.*

The lack of hard evidence supporting this legend has not stopped visitors and employees from having experiences with the ghost of Madeleine, who is blamed for most of the poltergeist-like activity that goes on there. The supposed portrait of Madeline is a focal point of paranormal activity. In an interview given to Barabra Sillery in her book *The Haunting of Mississippi*, tavern keeper Tom Miller said that Yvonne Scott went to a thrift shop one day and purchased a portrait of a Spanish-looking girl holding a red apple. She hung the portrait over the fireplace because it matched her conception of what Madeline would have looked like. "There are times when the picture is on the wall and it starts swinging violently back and forth," Miller said. Madeline's mischievous spirit has also been credited with causing a chain hanging from a wall to swing on its own.

Madeline's full-body apparition is believed by many to have made an appearance in King's Tavern in 1974. One day, a docent at one of the city's many antebellum homes dropped off her daughter at the front door so that she could sell Christmas cards to raise money for her high school drill team. The door was locked, so the girl walked around the outside of the building and looked through the windows. Suddenly, she ran back to her mother's car and jumped in the front seat. When her mother asked her what had happened, she replied that she was staring through one of the windows when she saw a young woman wearing a red rider's habit walking down the main stairs. She was wearing a hat and riding boots. The girl told her mother that the ghost remained visible for just a few seconds before disappearing.

Employees at King's Tavern also believe that Madeline's ghost seems to be especially fond of the upstairs rooms. Yvonne Scott said that when she first took over the tavern, she was discussing the plumbing with a friend upstairs when water started running out of a dead pipe. In the 1970s, a tavern employee named Beverly Franzen was upstairs all by herself when she heard a disembodied voice say, "Hello." In the 1980s, a young woman in the attic was looking into the mirror as she was putting on lipstick when, all at once, her image was replaced with that of a woman with red hair. On his first day as manager in 1977, Grover Moberly walked up to the third-floor bathroom, where he was surprised to find small, wet footprints the size of a woman's foot all over the floor. It appeared as if someone had just climbed out of the bathtub. Goosebumps rose on his arm when he noticed that the bathtub was covered with dirt and spiderwebs.

One of the other ghosts at King's Tavern makes its presence known through sound. In the early 1800s, Micajah "Big" Harpe was staying in the inn when he was awakened by the crying of a baby. He walked into the mail room, where a distraught woman was trying to rock a fussy infant to sleep. Big Harpe held out his arms and asked her if he could hold the baby. Grateful for the assistance, the woman handed the child over to him. Big Harpe then grabbed the baby by the ankles and swung it against the wall, smashing its skull. Employees and customers have often heard the cries of a baby throughout the tavern. An employee named Sonia Frost was putting crackers on the tables when she heard a baby crying. Tavern keeper Miller said that the sound of a baby crying has been heard at table number 11 and table number 12.

The ghostly image of a tall "man in black" has been seen standing near the fireplace in the dining room. *flickr.com.*

A number of people have seen the ghost of an Indian runner standing in front of the fireplace in the mail room. *flickr.com.*

The other two ghosts that haunt King's Tavern are males. Customers have photographed the image of a tall man wearing black clothes, a black string tie and a black top hat near the fireplace in the main dining room. A few people have felt a large hand gripping their shoulders and neck. Locals believe he may be the spirit of one of the many outlaws who spent their ill-gotten money at the tavern.

Another male ghost is the spirit of one of the Indian runners who delivered mail to King's Tavern in the eighteenth and nineteenth centuries. He has been sighted standing in the mail room staring out of a window facing the street. According to Danny Scott, his apparition has been seen at midnight standing in front of the fireplace in the mail room.

King's Tavern remains one of the city's best—and most popular—restaurants. It is known far and wide for its pot pies topped with biscuit crusts, wood-fired flatbreads and juicy steaks. According to the legends that still draw people here, one might also have an opportunity to sample spirits of the nonalcoholic variety.

MARY MAHONEY'S (BILOXI)

A French colonist named Louis Frazier erected the historic building locally known in Biloxi as the "Old French House" in 1737. The house was constructed with cypress columns, wooden pegs and hand-made bricks. The roof and the porch floor were made of slate imported from France. The Old French House was one of the only homes in Biloxi with a cellar. The Frazier family lived in the house until 1820, when it passed into the hands of a succession of different owners. Jean Baptiste Bienville, the colonial governor of the Louisiana Territory, used the home as his headquarters between 1701 and 1743. In 1962, Bob and Mary Mahoney and her brother Andrew Cvitanovich converted the old house into a restaurant. Over the next two years, the new owners took great pains to preserve the historical integrity of the house. The restaurant opened its doors for business in 1964 after the restoration was complete. Following the devastation caused by Hurricane Katrina in 2005, the old building had to be restored a second time. The surging water severely damaged the kitchen and the dining rooms. The heart pine floors were so warped that they had to be replaced for the first time since the 1700s. However, the structure of the house was still sound, so Mary Mahoney's was able to reopen after only nine weeks. Customers have traveled hundreds of miles to sample Mary Mahoney's French cuisine, steaks and seafood. Photographs of celebrities who have eaten there hang from the walls. Some people believe that the history of Mary Mahoney's also lives on in the spirits of the old house's former occupants.

Originally known as the Old French House when it was built in 1737, Mary Mahoney's is one of the finest restaurants in Biloxi. *Author's collection*.

A shadowy figure was sighted walking into the men's restroom in Mary Mahoney's. *Author's collection.*

The owners of the restaurant began to sense that something otherworldly was sharing the old house with them soon after the restaurant opened. Mary Mahoney's daughter, Eilene, said that one evening after closing, her parents were sitting in the kitchen when, all at once, pots and pans began falling off their hooks onto the floor. Not long thereafter, a customer who claimed to be a psychic told his server that a gang of redcoats were running across the room. In 2005, shortly before Hurricane Katrina, several cast members of the Lord of the Dance troupe were dining in the restaurant when one of them told his server that he saw a shadow figure walk through the door of the men's restroom next to the receptionist's station. One of the male servers entered the room, but nobody was there.

Mary Mahoney's is unique among haunted places in that the owners and staff believe they know the identity of their resident spirit. Her name is Angelique. She was the wife of a sailor who lived in a room on the second floor of the house. Angelique makes her presence known in Mary Mahoney's through poltergeist activity. Disembodied footsteps and bumping and banging sounds are usually attributed to her. To Angelique, the historic restaurant is not Mary Mahoney's; it is hers.

THE SPENGLER HOTEL (JACKSON)

The old Spengler Hotel in the Bellhaven district of Jackson has a fascinating history. When it was built in 1927 as a hotel for railroad men, Bellehaven Heights was still a nice residential area. In 1930, Louise Middleton sold the building to J.S. Miller, who converted it into Miller's Café. Humphries Barbershop was housed on the east corner of the building. After a few years, the name of the business was changed to Miller's Place. Guests could spend the night upstairs for thirty-five cents a night; lunch was served downstairs. Throughout the 1940s, J.W. Miller managed the upstairs; his wife, Louise, ran the café. In 1950, Herbert Stair bought the restaurant. The business changed hands again in 1954, when it became the GM&O Beanery. One year later, Hugh Tullo bought the restaurant. People say that in the 1940s and 1950s, prostitutes plied their trade in the upper rooms. In the early 1960s, the restaurant operated as the Spengler Street Café. After standing empty for a few years, the Central Systems Company opened up in the building in 1973. Photographer Steve Colston purchased the property in 1976 for use as a photography studio. Colston remained in the building for thirty-five years.

Soon after Steve Colston took over the property, he began hearing stories about the old hotel's violent past from people in the neighborhood. In the early years, one of the owners was found shot in the head in one of the upper bedrooms. The death was ruled a suicide, but most of the locals believe he was murdered. A shoot-out took place upstairs in the 1950s. One man was killed; the bullet holes were still visible in the wall when Colston moved in. In the 1930s, a man who had been having an affair with a married woman

The former Spengler Hotel was built in 1927 as a "beanery"—a hotel for railroad men. *Author's collection.*

returned drunk to the hotel one night. He was lying in bed, sleeping it off, when the woman's husband stormed in the room, dragged his wife's lover out of the bed and stomped his head with his boots, killing him.

Colston was fairly certain that the murdered man's ghost was responsible for most of the paranormal activity the he and his family experienced inside the building. Soon after buying the old hotel, Colston and his grandmother were restoring two of the lower rooms when she told him that someone was walking around upstairs. Her first thought was that it was Colston's grandfather. Colston replied that he was pretty sure that his grandfather was outside. The pair looked out a window and, sure enough, his grandfather was outside washing paint brushes. Colston checked upstairs, but no one was there. The disembodied footsteps continued for so long that Colston decided to muffle the sound by hiring a man to lay carpet upstairs. One evening, Coston and his wife returned to the studio after dining out and were surprised to find the carpet man sitting in his truck. He told them that their building was haunted and then went on to say that he heard voices while he was working, even though he knew that he was the only one there. Colston admitted that he had heard the voices too on occasion.

Other things happened in the former hotel that defy explanation. Frequently, the light fixtures fell down because the screws holding them to the beam came loose. Falling lights completely destroyed a camera and an enlarger. A man who managed a pottery shop upstairs complained that sometimes when he was in the bathroom, the doorknob would turn, as if someone was trying to get in. One evening, Colston heard the tinkling of a bell that was tied to a door leading to the outside stairs. When he opened the door and walked down the stairs, he suddenly felt a frigid wave wash over him. He was the only one there. On another occasion, a couple of men brought in a camera. While Colston was inspecting it, a Coke bottle that one of the men set down on the desk turned over and rolled off. The rowdy days of the railroad men and drinking and gambling may be long gone, but their psychic energy remains, imprinted in the walls of the Spengler Hotel.

THE OLD CAPITOL MUSEUM (JACKSON)

Construction of the Old State Capitol began in 1833, but work was halted because of inferior building materials. William Nichols replaced the original architect, John Lawrence, in 1836; Nichols completed the three-story building in 1839, using the Capitol building in Washington, D.C., as his inspiration.

Brick, stucco and limestone were used in the exterior of the structure. Most of the interior was made of wood, except for the brick partition walls. A ninety-four-foot-high copper rotunda dome was raised over the first floor. At the time of its completion, the Old State Capitol was the most imposing Greek Revival structure in the entire state.

A number of important events took place in the Old State Capitol in the nineteenth century, including the following:

> *A visit and address by Andrew Jackson in 1840.*
> *The passage of the Ordinance of Secession in 1861.*
> *The Constitutional Convention of 1865 after the fall of the Confederacy.*
> *The overthrow of carpetbag government by the Mississippi legislature of 1876.*
> *The last address of Jefferson Davis to the Mississippi legislature in 1884.*
> *The passage of a law establishing the first state-supported college for higher education of women in America, the Industrial Institute and College, in Columbus, Mississippi in 1884.*
> *The Constitutional Convention of 1890.*

The Old State Capitol was closed in 1903 after the completion of a new capitol. The building stood abandoned until it was renovated for use as office space for state officials in 1917. After state agencies moved to a different location in 1960, the Old State Capitol was renovated. It opened as the State Historical Museum the next year. The building served as the State Historical Museum from 1961 until 2005, when it became the Old Capitol Museum. In 1969, the building was added to the National Register of Historic Places. It became a National Historic Landmark in 1990.

Oftentimes, legends arise in the absence of logical explanations for strange phenomena. This might be the case with the Old Capitol Museum. For years, security guards walking through the building after hours have heard thumping, banging and hammering sounds on the walls, as well as the sound of doors opening and closing. At the time, the security guard was the only person inside. By the mid-twentieth century, these disturbances were blamed on the ghost of a nameless legislator who supposedly died of a heart attack inside the capitol building sometime in the 1800s. Because these noises are generally heard only at night, most visitors to the museum would probably never have heard them.

Another possible source for the disturbing sounds was suggested in Barbara Sillery's book *The Haunting of Mississippi* (2011). Ruth Cole,

The Old State Capitol served as the Mississippi statehouse from 1839 to 1903. It became the State Historical Museum in 1961. *Author's collection.*

who works as a hostess for the Old Capitol Museum, mentioned that the disembodied footsteps that some security guards have heard at night might be those of the ghost of Dr. Felix Underwood, who served as the director of the Bureau of Child Hygiene and Welfare between 1924 and 1958. Because of Dr. Underwood's dedication to the bureau, as well as the fact that he died of a heart attack while sitting at his desk, Cole admitted that he is the only person she could think of who might be walking the halls after death. Some of the sounds might indicate that the haunting activity in the Old Capitol Museum is residual. Several officers told Clay Williams, the museum director, that they heard thumping sounds coming from Underwood's former office, where he died. Dr. Underwood hit his head on his desk when he had his heart attack. Experts in the paranormal believe that this is the sound the security guards are hearing, played over and over again.

Clay Williams and Lucy Allen, the museum division director over all the state facilities, believe that at least some of the museum's ghost stories may have been generated by an exhibit consisting of the off-white figures of senators engaged in debate in the restored second-floor senate chamber. The exhibit is visible from one of the museum's windows. So, is the reported paranormal activity in the Old State Capitol real, or has it been fueled by weird unexplained noises and a ghostly exhibit?

MERREHOPE (MERIDIAN)

Merrehope is noteworthy, not only as one of the few buildings in Meridian to survive the Civil War, but also as one of the most striking antebellum homes in Mississippi. In 1831, Richard McLemore purchased seven hundred acres and built a house of logs and wooden pegs on what is now Eleventh Street and Eighteenth Avenue one year after the signing of the Treaty of Dancing Rabbit, which opened the Choctaw lands to settlement. In 1858, McLemore gave his daughter Juriah a Greek Revival cottage as a wedding gift. Over the years, the mansion now known as Merrehope blossomed from these humble antebellum beginnings.

During the Civil War, the Jacksons' home was taken over by both the Confederate and Union armies. In December 1863, the cottage became the family residence and the headquarters of Confederate general Leonidas Polk. Two months later, on February 14, General Polk was driven out of Meridian by William Tecumseh Sherman's army of ten thousand soldiers, who set fire to much of the city and destroyed all of the railroads in a ten-mile radius. Union officers reoccupied Polk's former headquarters.

Merrehope changed hands several times in the years following the war. In 1868, it was purchased by John Gary, a cotton broker, and his wife, Eliza, who built the main block of the house. Gary also added his own personal touches to the home, including the double parlor, the library and the four upstairs rooms, all designed in the Italianate style. In 1881, a coal dealer and Civil War veteran named J.C. Lloyd moved into Merrehope with his wife and thirteen children. He left his impact on his personal residence and on the city as a whole, founding the city's first school system and serving as city clerk. In 1903, another cotton broker named Sam Floyd from Shubuta became the proud owner of Merrehope. A very wealthy man, Floyd had the means to convert the large, homey residence into a more palatial structure. Using the neoclassical style, he added the front columns, the balcony, five bathrooms, the walnut stairway, the dining room, two upstairs servants' rooms and the morning room. A giant portico was added to the south and east sides of the building. In 1915, Merrehope was converted into rental

Richard McLemore built Merrehope in 1854 as a wedding present for his daughter Juriah. It served as the headquarters for Confederate general Leonidas Polk in 1864. During the Battle of Meridian, General William Tecumseh Sherman's officers stayed here as well. *Author's collection.*

property. In the 1930s, it was divided into eight apartments. Merrehope was being used as a boardinghouse when the Meridian Restorations Foundation purchased it in 1968 and named it "Merrehope," a combination of "Meridian Restorations" and "hope." Merrehope was added to the National Register of Historic Places in 1971; in 1995, the structure was designated a Mississippi Landmark.

Reports of paranormal activity inside Merrehope surfaced not long after the mansion was opened to the public. The first ghost to make its presence known was the spirit of Eugenia Gary, the daughter of John Gary, who moved to Meridian from Livingston in 1868. Even though Eugenia and her sister Pristinia died of tuberculosis at the end of the Civil War and were buried in Alabama, Eugenia seems to have formed a special attachment to the beautiful house that she never occupied while alive. Fonda Rush, former historical preservationist for the City of Meridian, recalled her first encounter with Eugenia, Merrehope's "friendly" ghost, a few days before she started working there as a hostess: "This was 1973, and I was just coming out of college. [I was] dating this boy…from the Navy, and I had told him about Merrehope, so we drove over there, and we came up on opposite sides of the house. But I came around the corner on the porch, and he went around the front of the house. He mentioned that he had seen my shadow, but the light was off. It couldn't have been my shadow. About that time, Merrehope was being restored, and they didn't have the lace curtains on the windows yet, and you could look, and there she [a female figure] stood, in the center of the room, looking at us."

Since Fonda's sighting, other people have seen the ghost of Eugenia Gary at Merrehope, including Fonda's daughter. In 1992, during a Halloween party, Fonda's daughter and several of her friends were dressed in period clothes, greeting the guests who were attending a national mangers' meeting at Merrehope for one of Meridian's large corporations. "My daughter was standing on the balcony outside of the Museum Room, where Eugenia's portrait is," Fonda said. "She felt like somebody was watching her. She turned around, and Eugenia was standing in the window." That same night, a young African American man who lived in the neighborhood was walking home, and he too saw a figure he described as "a lady in a long dress" standing in the same window.

Over the years, Eugenia's ghost has manifested in a number of different ways. Docents reported hearing disembodied footsteps in different parts of the house. Fonda said that furniture placed in one part of the house appeared in an entirely different room the next morning: "I'd leave work, and when I'd come back, there'd be a chair sitting in the middle of the hallway for no reason. And I'd call everyone I knew who had keys, and no one had been over there."

Fonda believes that it was not coincidence that Eugenia's spirit became active inside the house not long after the portraits of her and her sister were donated to the Merrehope Foundation. "In 1969, when hurricane Camille hit, the portraits were damaged by the hurricane, and we had them sent off to the Mississippi University for Women to have one of their professors look at restoring the portraits. While they were up there, nothing happened.…All activity stopped…for seven months. And then when [the portraits] came back, everything started all over again, so I think that she goes with the portrait."

Former docent Donna White recalled one particular night when a group of senior citizens accidentally gathered photographic evidence of Eugenia's presence during the Trees of Merrehope event. "They took pictures downstairs in the double parlor of the Christmas trees. They didn't see her

People passing by have seen Merrehope's friendly spirit, Eugenia, standing in the window of the room where her portrait hangs. *Author's collection.*

A group of senior citizens accidentally took a photograph of Eugenia's ghost standing next to the Christmas tree in the double parlor. *Author's collection.*

then, but after they got the film developed, they could see her! She was standing there beside the tree!"

Donna White's only sighting of Eugenia occurred one evening in 2010 when she had just walked through the double parlor into the main hall. All at once, she caught a glimpse of a female figure walking away from her toward the back of the house. As she stood there, shaking, Donna called out, "Eugenia." She sensed immediately that she was all alone once again. Afterward, Donna regretted seeing only Eugenia's backside and not her face.

On the other hand, Donna did not look forward to ever meeting up with the male ghost that haunts the Periwinkle Room, also known as the "Suicide Room." In the 1930s, when Merrehope was divided into apartments, the Periwinkle Room was rented by a retired teacher who most likely suffered from a bipolar disorder. One night, he had several of his friends over to his room to play poker. By the time the game was over, the room was filled with the odor of cigar smoke and bourbon. After the last guest had left the house, the man picked up several of the empty whiskey bottles and lined them up on the mantle above the fireplace. He then picked up his pistol and began shooting the bottles. As soon as the last bottle had shattered, the man placed the gun to his temple and fired, blowing out his brains. Eventually, the holes in the mantle were filled with putty but were still partially visible.

Because of the Periwinkle Room's tragic past, a number of docents have been reluctant to go inside. Fonda Rush believes that the paranormal presence inside the Periwinkle Room is almost palpable: "In his room, sometimes you can smell cigar-cigarette smoke.…His room also can be extremely cold sometimes. And his footsteps—you can hear him moving, but his footsteps are heavier. But he never seems to leave that room. [On the other hand], Eugenia seems to move around." Fonda added that the teacher's ghost is much scarier to her than is Eugenia's spirit, which is why she and the other docents are reluctant to talk about him.

Donna White found out how frightening the teacher's ghost can be just a few weeks after she started working, when she had her first paranormal experience in the antebellum home. One evening, Donna straightened out the bed covers in the Periwinkle Room, just as she had been doing every day before going home. The next morning, Donna stepped into the room and was shocked by what she saw. There on the bed was the clear imprint of a human body. Donna said it looked like someone had been lying there all night. The ladies assured her that this sort of thing happened all the

The Periwinkle Room is haunted by the angry spirit of a retired schoolteacher who shot himself there following a poker game. Docents have found the imprint of a body on the bed when they open up in the morning. *Author's collection.*

time in the "Suicide Room." Later that year, Donna became accustomed to hearing loud noises coming from the room: "I would come up here [to the Periwinkle Room], thinking something [had] fallen and glass [had] broken, but it was nothing."

Unlike many of the ladies who have given tours at Merrehope, docent Faye Johnson has not had a paranormal encounter of her own in Merrehope, except for hearing a few strange sounds: "I hear footsteps upstairs sometimes. It sounds like it's coming from the hallway." However, she has spoken to a number of people who have had encounters with Merrehope's "friendly spirit." In 2017, a man arrived at Merrehope on a Diamond Tour Bus. He walked into the gift shop and asked Hilda Roberts where the young woman was who had greeted him at the front door. He said he spoke a few words to her before she turned away and walked inside. Her curiosity aroused, Hilda asked him to describe the girl. He said she had long, brown hair and wore a long dress with a green vest. The man was noticeably shocked when Hilda told him that the girl was probably Merrehope's resident spirit. "He became very angry and said that he did not believe in ghosts," Faye said. "About fifteen minutes later, a woman who had ridden on the same bus told Hilda that the man thought that someone was playing a trick on him. She then added that she believed in ghosts."

Faye Johnson is like many people who spend considerable time in a haunted house and become attached to the spirits. "Over the past summer [2019], I was afraid that Eugenia had 'passed over' and was gone because I had not heard her or sensed her presence in the house for quite a while," Faye said. "This past October, the leader of a ghost hunting group from Vicksburg that were investigating Merrehope told me that Eugenia is still here and is looking out for the house."

ROSSWOOD PLANTATION (LORMAN)

Rosswood Plantation is a Greek Revival antebellum plantation on Highway 532 between Lorman and Red Lick in Jefferson County. It was built in 1857 on 1,285 acres of land by David Shroder, a master mechanic from Rodney, for Dr. Walter Ross Wade (1810–1862). The purchase price was $10,000. Although legend has it that Dr. Wade had the house built for his second wife, Mabelle Chamberlain Wade, it was actually built two and a half years before their marriage. Following Dr. Wade's death in 1862, the property was divided among his family members, with his wife inheriting the mansion and 100 acres. On July 4 and 5, 1864, during the Battle of Coleman's Plantation and the Battle of the Cotton Bales, Rosswood suffered severe damage to the kitchen from Union artillery. For a short time, Rosswood served as a field hospital for the Union and Confederate armies. Mabelle Wade cared for many dying and wounded soldiers. In 1898, Mary E. Hamer, a niece of Confederate president Jefferson Davis, acquired the home, which became known as the Hamer House. The house was sold during the Great Depression and had a number of owners in the following years, including Mr. and Mrs. Daniel Mason, who made extensive repairs, and Mr. and Mrs. Douglass Black, who added a number of modern amenities. In 1976, the house was bought by its present owners, Colonel and Mrs. Walter R. Hylander, who converted it into a bed-and-breakfast. The cash crop has switched over from cotton to Christmas trees. Rosswood became a private residence in 2019.

Ghost legends abound in Rosswood. For years, people have seen the ghost of one of the Union soldiers who died in the house in 1864. He is said to be a very friendly spirit who says "Hello" to visitors. In the room in back of the house, people have heard the giggling of little girls. The most frequently sighted ghost at Rosswood is the spirit of Mabelle Wade. In 2013, Carol Murdock had an encounter with a female spirit in one of the bedrooms that is reputed to be haunted: "As I came upon the dresser, I saw a full-bodied apparition of a woman in the mirror. She was standing between the sofa and bed looking toward the mirror. I turned around toward the sofa to look and she vanished! She was in Victorian dress with dark hair piled on top of her head. She appeared to be late 30s—early 40s in age." Although she was told by Jean Hylander that this may have been the ghost of Mabelle Wade, Carol Murry believes that the specter may have been the ghost of Mary Elizabeth Davis Mitchell Hamer, because her clothes were from a later time period.

In July 2016, my wife, Marilyn, and I spent the night in this same room at Rosswood Plantation. In the afternoon, we walked through the room, hoping to catch an orb or two on our cameras, but the spirits did not cooperate. Later that evening, we returned to our room after dinner and attempted to communicate with the ghost using a Maglite flashlight. I barely turned off the flashlight and placed it on the fireplace mantle. I then told the spirit to turn on the flashlight if the answer to my question was "Yes." For the next five minutes, Marilyn and I had a lively conversation with the ghost in the room, who answered questions like, "Were you happy living in Rosswood?" by turning on the flashlight. Although our experience is certainly not definitive proof that Rosswood is haunted, it certainly was unusual, especially because I have tried to reach out to the spirits in other supposedly haunted inns using the same method with no results at all.

THE WINDSOR RUINS (PORT GIBSON)

A wealthy cotton planter named Smith Coffee Daniell II built Windsor Plantation facing the Mississippi River on his 2,600-acre farm. When construction began in 1859, Daniell intended for his magnificent Greek Revival home to be the most splendid house in the area. The seventeen-thousand-square-foot mansion had twenty-nine forty-foot fluted Corinthian columns, wide verandas, a doctor's office, a library, a school room and over twenty rooms, each with its own marble fireplace. Daniell supervised his crew of carpenters, plasterers and brick masons, who had been recruited from Mississippi, the northeastern states and Europe. When construction was completed in 1861, building costs had risen to $175,000. Windsor Plantation soon attracted visitors from far and wide. Mark Twain is said to have spent the night here while piloting his steamship down the Mississippi River just before the Civil War. Unfortunately, Daniell did not live long enough to enjoy his showplace. He died of a heart attack on April 12, 1861, only a few weeks after construction was completed.

During the Civil War, Windsor soldiers watched for Union troops from the mansion's cupola. In 1863, just before Grant's Vicksburg campaign, Union soldiers interrupted a large ball that was being held at Windsor Plantation and arrested three Confederate soldiers, despite the vigorous objection from the ladies. After Grant began to move on Vicksburg, ten thousand Union troops landed just west of Windsor at the port of Bruinsburg. They took over the mansion on April 29, 1863, for use as an observation and signal station and as a field hospital. One Union soldier was shot and killed in the front doorway of the plantation home. General Grant was so angry that he planned to take revenge by burning down the mansion, but Catherine Daniell talked the soldiers into burning the barn instead. Over four hundred soldiers were treated at Windsor during its tenure as a field hospital. Approximately thirty soldiers were buried on the grounds.

The apparition of a Union soldier has been seen at the Windsor Ruins, which were destroyed by fire on February 17, 1890. *Author's collection.*

Following the Civil War, the Daniell family resumed their privileged lifestyle. For the next twenty years, Windsor Plantation was the social center of Port Gibson. Although the family had lost a considerable amount of money during the war, leasing out their landholdings provided a steady source of income. Everything changed, however, on February 17, 1890. At 10:30 a.m., a young man threw his cigarette into a pile of trash left by carpenters who were making repairs. Within minutes, the house was ablaze. The family lost most of its possessions, including the elegant furniture, jewelry, the library and household furnishings. Only the balustrades, columns, cast-iron stairways and pieces of bone china survived the fire.

After the fire, Catherine and her family moved to a plantation they called "Retreat." By the time she died in 1903 at age seventy-three, Catherine had lived in her new home for thirteen years. The property was passed down to her daughter, Priscilla, who married Joseph Magruder. In 1974, their descendants donated 2.1 acres, including the Windsor ruins, to the state of Mississippi. The site includes twenty-three complete columns and five partial columns. All of the cast-iron stairways have been removed. The still imposing remnants of one of the South's greatest homes have been used in the films *Raintree County* (1957) starring Elizabeth Taylor and Montgomery Clift and *The Ghosts of Mississippi* (1996) starring Alec Baldwin and Whoopi Goldberg.

The Windsor ruins project a spectral presence in their lonely vigil over the landscape. Many visitors have reported hearing the faint strains of dance music and laughter wafting through the air. The apparition of a Union soldier has been sighted standing guard at the spot where the front door once stood. Some people believe this is the ghost of the Yankee who was killed after Grant's army took control of the plantation house. The most active ghost is the spirit of a man in nineteenth-century attire that strolls across the grounds. Many witnesses believe it is the pensive apparition of Smith Coffee Daniell, who was denied his right to live out a full life at the Windsor Plantation. His apparition is so clear and lifelike that a number of visitors have walked over to speak to him.

VICKSBURG NATIONAL BATTLEFIELD (VICKSBURG)

President Abraham Lincoln was convinced from the very beginning of the Civil War that the most strategic city on the Mississippi River was Vicksburg: "The Red River in Louisiana and the Arkansas and White rivers in Arkansas both emptied into the Mississippi and could be used for shipping Confederate supplies," Lincoln said. "From Vicksburg, these supplies can be distributed by rail all over the Confederacy." Lincoln believed that because of all the goods that filtered down the Mississippi into Vicksburg from the Delta farmland, it was a key Confederate city. "The war can never be brought to a close until that key is in our pocket," Lincoln said. He was also fully aware that of all the points on the river, Vicksburg would be the most difficult to conquer.

Grant officially began his siege of Vicksburg on May 25, 1863, by ordering his engineers to dig siege trenches as well as a series of tunnels under Confederate fortifications. Grant had planned to fill the tunnels with explosives and ignite them, thereby blowing up the fortifications. Admiral David Porter's gunboats bombarded the city. Soon after Confederate general John Pemberton positioned his army inside the defenses, the populace of Vicksburg moved out of their homes. For most of the forty-seven-day siege, people lived in dugouts and caves in the hills. Men, women and children left their shelters just long enough to search for food while the Union artillerymen

Inside the visitors center at the Vicksburg National Military Park is a reproduction of one of the dugout caves where people took shelter during the siege. *Author's collection.*

ate their meals. Bread, sugar, coffee, beef and even horse and mule meat were almost impossible to find. Some people resorted to eating dogs and rats. The soldiers' diet was not much better. Many of them had only four ounces of rotted bacon, a biscuit and a little rice for their daily rations.

On June 25, the tunnel under the Third Louisiana Redoubt was detonated, blowing off the entire top of the hill. The invading Union forces who poured into the crater were surprised to find that not only had the Confederates already left the redoubt, but also that they were firing down on them from the top of the crater. By the time the fighting ended, between three hundred and four hundred of Grant's soldiers were killed or wounded. General Pemberton reported a loss of ninety men.

However, the end of the Confederate defense of Vicksburg was rapidly approaching. By June 2, the Union trenches had moved so close to the Confederate army that the soldiers only had time for one volley before being driven back. Approximately half of General Pemberton's soldiers had been stricken with disease, including gangrene and dysentery. On July 3, 1863, flags of truce were raised along the line of trenches while Grant

Visitors crossing the battlefield have heard the spectral "boom" of cannon fire. *Author's collection.*

and Pemberton worked out the terms of surrender. The Confederate defenders of the city were ordered to surrender their arms, but they were paroled instead of being sent to prison. On July 4, General Pemberton ordered his divisions to march to the surrender point. Grant's losses amounted to 1,514 killed, 7,395 wounded, and 453 captured or missing. Confederate records indicate that 1,260 were killed, 3,572 were wounded and 4,227 were missing or captured.

Vicksburg National Military Park is similar to other Civil War battlefields in that the war is not over for all of the Union and Confederate soldiers. Many tourists claim to have detected the odor of gunpowder on the battlefield. Smoke from indeterminate sources occasionally wafts from the air. People have heard the boom of distant cannons on days when no reenactors are present. Even more unsettling are the agonized screams of men and horses that send shivers up the spines of visitors. One young man who had just gotten off work at the casino was jogging around the Vicksburg National Cemetery when he saw a bank of fog hovering over several graves. The fog appeared nowhere else in the cemetery. On another occasion, a visitor was walking up to the spot where Confederate forces drove back an assault by Union forces when he, too, saw a cloud of fog. It was thirty yards long and ten yards wide. Even more unsettling was the fact that the fog was moving against the wind.

Specific monuments in the park are said to be haunted as well. The best known is the Pennsylvania Monument. It is said that when someone shines a flashlight on the faces on the five medallions at night, the eyes blink. Visitors have reported seeing smoke drifting out of the muzzle of the cannon in front of the Texas Memorial. Ghostly Union soldiers have been sighted around the Illinois Memorial, usually near the Third Louisiana Redan. Like many casualties of war, these men probably died so quickly and violently that their spirits are in a state of confusion, unsure as to whether they are dead or alive.

5

LEGENDARY CHARACTERS

THE PHANTOM BARBER OF PASCAGOULA
(PASCAGOULA)

The year 1942 was a time of pivotal change for the United States as a whole and for the state of Mississippi in particular. Because of its proximity to the Gulf of Mexico, the tiny town of Pascagoula became a center for warship construction. Within the span of just a few months, Pascagoula's population swelled from five thousand to fifteen thousand. Needless to say, the huge influx of workers disrupted the tranquility of Pascagoula. Most of the crimes took the form of barroom brawls. One crime spree, however, still has many locals scratching their heads.

On Friday, June 5, 1942, two young girls—Edna Maria Maree Hydel and Evelyn Briggs—had just fallen asleep in their room at the Our Lady of Victories convent when they were awakened by the sound of a man climbing out of their bedroom window. Nothing was taken except for a lock of hair from each girl's head. The next morning, Mary told authorities that the intruder was "sorta short, sorta fat, and…wearing a white sweatshirt."

The Phantom Barber, as he came to be known, struck again the following Monday. Six-year-old Carol Peattie was sleeping next to her twin brother when someone cut away the screen from the bedroom window, climbed in and shore off a lock of her hair. The only clue left behind was a single sandy footprint beneath the window.

Although the nature of the "thefts" linked the two home intrusions, investigators were unable to make a positive identification. One week after the break-in at the convent, someone cut the bathroom screen in the house owned by Mr. and Mrs. T. Heidelberg and proceeded to beat the sleeping couple with a heavy iron bar. This time, no hair was cut off, but Mrs. Heidelberg lost two front teeth. The Heidelbergs survived their vicious attack but were unable to describe their assailant because they had been beaten unconscious. The police used dogs to track down a pair of bloody gloves that had been discarded. Police theorized that the Barber had escaped on a bicycle.

The final "midnight visitation" took place two weeks later on a Sunday night. Mrs. R.R. Taylor was awakened by the nauseating odor of something being pressed over her face. When she regained consciousness, Mrs. Taylor discovered that the Phantom Barber had made off with a lock of her hair. Police determined that the Phantom Barber had anesthetized Taylor with a rag soaked in chloroform.

Even though the residents of Pascagoula continued talking about the nocturnal attacks for weeks after the intrusion in Mrs. Taylor's home, the Phantom Barber made no more appearances. Two months after the Barber chloroformed Taylor, the police arrested a fifty-seven-year-old German chemist named William Dolan. Evidence connecting Dolan with the Phantom Barber included a bundle of human hair found on Dolan's property. Some of the hair was traced back to Carol Peattie. The fact that Dolan held a grudge against Mr. Heidelberg's father, a magistrate, suggested that revenge may have been the primary motive in the brutal assault. Dolan submitted a plea of innocence during his trial. He was found guilty of attempted murder and sentenced to ten years in prison. He was released from prison in 1951 after passing a lie detector test.

In the public's mind, Dolan was the Phantom Barber, although he was never charged with any of the home invasions. Some researchers familiar with the case believe that Dolan may have been caught up in the paranoia that was sweeping through the country at the time. Dolan's place of birth—Germany—branded him as the enemy in the minds of many residents of Pascagoula. Some people have even suggested that someone planted the hair behind his house in order to frame him. No more incidents of the Phantom Barber have occurred since Dolan's arrest.

ROBERT JOHNSON'S MYSTERIOUS LIFE AND DEATH (CLARKSDALE)

Robert Johnson was born on May 8, 1911, in Hazlehurst, Mississippi. He learned how to play guitar from Isaiah "Ike" Zimmerman after moving to Martinsville. After marrying Caletta Craft in May 1931, he and his wife moved to Clarksdale. Following Caletta's death in childbirth in 1932, he drifted between Memphis and Helena and a number of small towns in between, playing his music in juke joints and on street corners. He recorded twenty-nine songs in Jackson, Mississippi, around 1936 and in Dallas, Texas, in 1937. He died on August 16, 1938. Two important aspects of his life are shrouded in mystery.

The most famous legend associated with Robert Johnson concerns his playing ability. Bluesman Son House recalled that, as a boy, Johnson could play harmonica, but he was a very poor guitarist. After Johnson moved from Robinson to Martinsville, Mississippi, he was mentored by Zimmerman, who was said to have acquired his guitar-playing prowess by practicing at graveyards at night. After Johnson returned to Robinson, his guitar skills had improved immensely, giving rise to the devil legend. The story goes that Johnson took his guitar to a crossroads at the Dockery Plantation, where he met the devil. The dark figure tuned Johnson's guitar, played it for a while and returned it to the young man. The devil told Johnson that he would be granted mastery of the guitar in exchange for his immortal soul. The details of the story have been embellished over the years through various retellings. For example, in one version, Johnson sells his soul in a graveyard instead of at the crossroads. Some scholars believe the legend arose out of Johnson's fascination with the devil, which can be found in songs like "Cross Roads Blues" and "Hell Hound on My Trail."

According to legend, bluesman Robert Johnson gained the ability to play the guitar after selling his soul to the devil at the crossroads. *Wikimedia Commons.*

The various circumstances surrounding Johnson's death are mysterious as well. After Johnson died on August 16, 1938, near Greenwood, Mississippi, no cause of death was listed on his death certificate, giving rise to a number of different theories. Some scholars believe that the medical examiner assumed that Johnson died because he had syphilis. The most commonly told story involves a woman whom Johnson flirted with at a dance. According to Sonny Boy Williamson, she gave him a bottle of whiskey that had been poisoned by her husband. Three days later, Johnson died in great pain. A medical theory was proposed in 1996 by David Connell, who speculated that Johnson may have died from heart problems caused by Marfan syndrome.

THE BOY PROPHET OF HAZLEHURST (HAZLEHURST)

Just before sunrise on January 23, 1969, an F4 tornado cut a swath from Jefferson to Newton County. Hardest hit were Simpson and Copiah Counties, specifically, the African American community of Hazlehurst. Thirty-two people died and two hundred people were injured. The National Weather Service ranked it as the fifth-deadliest tornado in Mississippi history. It has taken years for the citizens to recover from the suffering and destruction caused by the tornado. Among the most unforgettable stories to emerge from the catastrophe is the visitation by a child who has come to be known as the "Boy Prophet of Hazlehurst."

Three years before the tornado struck, a strange little ten-year-old boy appeared on the streets of Hazlehurst. He had curly black hair, dark skin and an indentation on the top of his head where he placed a Coke bottle on his walks downtown. One of his eyes was crossed. Shirley Sandifer, who was six years old when the tornado picked up her home and set it down on the ground, said that people did not take the boy very seriously when he "preached that the Lord was going to bring something to Hazlehurst that was going to change their lives. People just chucked him aside and laughed at him." Other residents of Hazlehurst recalled that he possessed very unusual abilities. Shirley Watkins Little heard that the little boy had the power to heal. Some people say that when the police apprehended him and tried to take him to jail on the charge of vagrancy, the boy easily removed the handcuffs and escaped. Residents claim that they actually saw the boy leap from a tall wooden bridge and land lightly on the ground with no apparent injuries. One eyewitness recalled that the boy's legs seemed to be moving as he fell, almost as if he was walking in the air.

On January 23, 1969, many people who lost their homes and loved ones remembered the boy's unsettling prophecy. Approximately one hundred buildings were obliterated; over nine hundred people had nowhere to live. Many of the homeless residents moved away from Hazlehurst.

In the absence of immediate relief from state and national agencies, the people helped each other. Men and women even resorted to making stew from the blackbirds that lived in the sugarcane fields. Some people searched for the strange little boy who had predicted the tornado, but he was nowhere to be found.

Filmmaker Steve Collins, whose family survived the tornado, is filming a documentary on the boy prophet, whose fascinating story has intrigued Collins all of his life. Collins recalled that some people abused the little boy verbally and physically, throwing bottles at him and calling him names: "However, others took pity on him, giving him food and a place to spend the night." He believes that the police arrested the little boy primarily to keep him from harm. After interviewing approximately one hundred people, Collins has concluded that most of the residents of Hazlehurst view the boy prophet as a myth. He hopes that his completed documentary will reveal the truth about the strange little boy.

WHERE WAS JIMMIE RODGERS REALLY BORN?
(MERIDIAN)

The facts of Jimmie Rodgers's life are a matter of public record. According to most accounts of his life, he was born in Meridian, Mississippi, on September 8, 1897, the youngest son of a railroad man. He began working as a brakeman on the railroad when he was fourteen years old. Even though Rodgers was diagnosed with tuberculosis in 1924, he formed a musical trio with Slim Rozell and his sister-in-law, Elsie McWilliams. He also sang in medicine shows. Rodgers continued working on the railroad until he contracted a pulmonary hemorrhage in 1925. After being fired from the railroad, Rodgers devoted all of his time to his musical career. He and his family lived with the diagnosis for two years before moving to Johnson City, Tennessee. When his musical group, the Tenneva Ramblers, broke up, Rodgers went solo, recording two songs for RCA, "The Soldier's Sweetheart" and "Sleep, Baby, Sleep." Rogers recorded four more songs in November 1927. His song "Blue Yodel" is one of only a few country songs to sell one million copies. Rodgers finally achieved stardom in 1929, but at the expense of his health. After collapsing in February 1933, he scheduled a final recording session in May. Two days later, Rodgers died of a lung hemorrhage. He was thirty-five years old.

Jimmie Rodgers was buried in the Oak Grove Baptist Church graveyard in Meridian, the official place of his birth in 1933. *Author's collection.*

Unlike Robert Johnson, whose final resting place has never been determined with certainty, Jimmie Rodgers's grave is not up to speculation. He was buried next to his wife, Carrie, in Oak Grove Cemetery in Meridian, Mississippi. Controversy, though, surrounds his place of birth. According to the Jimmie Rodgers Museum website, Rodgers was born in Meridian. However, the Alabama Hall of Fame website lists his place of birth as Geiger, Alabama, the home of his paternal grandparents. The Encyclopedia of Alabama website takes a neutral stand on the controversy. Some say he was born in Meridian; others claim Geiger. Rodgers himself "muddied the waters" by signing documents later in life stating that he was born in Geiger. In his book *Jimmie Rodgers: The Life and Times of America's Blue Yodeler* (1992), biographer Nolan Porterfield says that Rodgers was born in Pine Springs, Mississippi, just north of Meridian. Unless new information is found, we may never know Jimmie Rodgers's true birthplace.

6

NATIVE AMERICAN LEGENDS

THE SINGING RIVER (PASCAGOULA)

One of the primary functions of legends is to explain natural phenomena. A good example can be found in Pascagoula, Mississippi. The eighty-mile-long Pascagoula River is America's largest free-flowing river. For many years, people boating, fishing or swimming in the Pascagoula River have heard a strange humming or buzzing sound, which has spawned the river's most famous legend.

One of the earliest versions of the tale, written by Governor Étienne Périer of French Louisiana, concerns a mermaid who lived in the river. The Pascagoula people, whose name means "bread eaters," worshiped an idol of the mermaid in their temple, praying and singing to it every night. Their lives changed forever with the arrival of Hernando de Soto's expedition (1539–40). A priest who accompanied the explorers immediately set about to convert the idolaters to Christianity. One day, a tower of water rose out of the river. On top of it stood the mermaid, who sang out to the people, inviting them to "come to me." Every member of the tribe was entranced by the mesmerizing tones of her song. One by one, they walked into the river, where their ghosts live in the underwater palace of the mermaid.

The best-known explanation for the "singing river" and the mysterious disappearance of the Pascagoula tribe involves a neighboring tribe, the Biloxi. Centuries ago, the Biloxi and Pascagoula tribes lived harmoniously along the waterways of Mississippi and Louisiana. This peaceful

Rather than be held in slavery by their enemies, the Pascagoula people chanted as they marched to their death into the Pascagoula River. Their singing can still be heard on the river today. *Author's collection.*

coexistence was shattered when the chief of the Pascagoula tribe, Altama, fell in love with the Biloxi princess, Anola. Fully aware of the ramifications of their love affair, they were nevertheless convinced that they could not live without each other. The Biloxi expressed their outrage by declaring war on the Pascagoula, who were clearly outnumbered. Rather than endure lives of slavery, the Pascagoula people decided to end their lives. One day, men, women and children marched into the Pascagoula River while singing their death song. Visitors and locals claim that their chanting can still be heard to this day.

According to other oral traditions, the Pascagoula tribe intermarried with other tribes in Texas and Louisiana. However, it is the romantic explanation of the disappearance of the Pascagoula people that still resonates with us today. In 1985, the Pascagoula River was renamed the Singing River by a county resolution.

THE LEGEND OF NANIH WAIYA MOUND (WINSTON COUNTY)

Nanih Waiya is an ancient rectangular platform mound in southern Winston County. Nanih Waiya is a Choctaw Indian name meaning "leaning hill." Measuring 25 feet tall and 220 feet wide, the mound was built in the Middle Woodland period between CE 300 and 600. The area was probably occupied until at least CE 700. At one time, the mound was enclosed by a raised embankment about 10 feet high, which has been destroyed by cultivation with the exception of a small portion lying along the edge of a swamp northwest of the mound. Over time, the mound has eroded into its present shape. The Choctaw people have been making pilgrimages to the site since the seventeenth century. The mound was preserved by the state of Mississippi for many years. Then, in 2006, the Mississippi legislature returned control of the site to the Luke family, which, in turn, deeded the property to the Mississippi Band of Choctaw Indians in 2006.

Legend has it that the Hopewell people were led by a medicine stick to a special place in southern Winston County. They buried the bones of their ancestors in the Nanih Waiya Mound. *Wikimedia Commons.*

A number of legends have been spawned by what the Choctaws called the "Mother Mound." This area just south of Tupelo was originally inhabited between AD 200 and 500 by bands of paleo Indians belonging to the Hopewell culture. According to Hopewell legends, their ancestors fled to this area from Mexico, bringing with them the bones of their ancestors. When the bands of Indians were on their way to the area around the Witch Dance, they were accompanied by a white dog, which led them to berries and food. The direction they took every morning was determined by a medicine stick. Every morning, the stick was found leaning to the east. Their journey ended when the stick stood straight up. Once the Indians had settled in the area, they buried the bones of their ancestors in a mound. As time passed, the leaders realized that they would eventually have to move to an area that had the resources to support their growing numbers. One of these leaders, Chata, remained in the mound area with half of the bands. A different leader, Chickasaw, took the other bands to the north, where they became known as the Chickasaw. In two variants of the origin story, the Choctaws emerged from Nanih Waiya or from a nearby cave.

THE RING IN THE OAK (BILOXI)

The Church of the Redeemer was the first Protestant church in Biloxi. The original church, erected in 1874, was moved to property donated by Harry T. Howard on Beach Boulevard and Bellman Street in 1891. In 1892, Howard erected a new church on the site; the old church was repurposed as the parish hall. The "new church" was destroyed by Hurricane Camille on August 17, 1969; the "old church" suffered considerable damage. With the assistance of men from Keesler Air Force Base, who cleaned up the mud and debris, the "old church" was remodeled and repaired by the end of the year. However, on August 29, 2005, the "old church" was completely destroyed by Hurricane Katrina. Today, many residents know the site as the location of the Hurricane Katrina Memorial and the place where the four-hundred-year-old oak tree that is the focus of the origin legend of the Ring in the Oak can be found.

The first written version of the legend of the Ring in the Oak was a poem by Laura F. Hinsdale titled "The Live Oak Ring"; it was published in 1896 in *Legends and Lyrics of the Gulf Coast*. In her version of the tale, a young warrior from the Natchez tribe and a princess from the Biloxi tribe fell in

The reputed four-hundred-year-old Ring in the Oak Tree can be found near the Hurricane Katrina Memorial in Biloxi. *Artwork courtesy of Benjamin Shadden.*

love. One day, he sought an audience with her father and showed him the ring that he had planned to give to the chief's daughter in marriage. The chief looked down at the ring and gave his conditions for the marriage. He told the young man that he could not marry his daughter until a ring formed in a nearby oak tree. A few months later, nature showed its approval of the union when a fierce storm forced two of the oak tree's branches to intertwine in the form of a ring.

The details of the tale evolved over the years through various reprintings and retellings. Then, on December 6, 1936, the *Times-Picayune* published what has become the definitive version. Through the miracle of the formation of a ring in an oak tree, the warring Pascagoula and Biloxi tribes are brought together. Like the giant oak tree that has weathered centuries of storms and hurricanes, the enduring love of the two young people has withstood the test of time.

THE LITTLE PEOPLE
(MISSISSIPPI CHOCTAW INDIAN RESERVATION)

Ireland's Leprechauns are probably the best-known little people, but these diminutive creatures can be found in countries all over the world, including Greece, New Zealand, Indonesia, the Hawaiian Islands and the Philippines. North America has its little people as well, such as the Nunnupi of the Comanche, the Jogahoh of the Iroquois, and the Ishigaq of the Inuit. For generations, Choctaws living in Mississippi told tales of the Kowi Anukasha, or "Forest Dwellers."

The Choctaw believed that the Kowi Anukasha kidnapped small children from their villages to see if they had the qualities of a tribal medicine man. Boys two, three or four years of age were grabbed by a watcher called "Kwanokasha" while they were playing in the woods. The boys were whisked away to a cave, where they were greeted by three spirits with long white hair. The boys were told they could have one of three gifts: a knife, poisonous herbs or medicinal herbs. Only the boys who selected the good herbs were groomed to become tribal doctors. For the boys' time in the cave, the three spirits revealed the secrets of tapping the medicinal properties of herbs, roots and the bark of specific trees. The spirits also taught the boys which of these "medicines" could be used to treat pain and diseases.

Three days later, the boys were returned unharmed to the villages. Before they were released, the three spirits told the boys to never tell anyone what they had seen or heard in the cave. Once the boys had grown up and become medicine men, they still kept the source of their knowledge a secret. Only the tribal doctors had the ability to see the Kowi Anukasha, who communicated with them and assisted them. The Choctaw believed that, sometimes at night, the medicine man and the Kowi Anukasha took the form of a light that darted through the woods in search of specific herbal remedies.

7

LOST TREASURE LEGENDS

CHIEF TOBY TUBBY'S BURIED GOLD
(COLLEGE HILL)

One of Mississippi's most colorful characters in the nineteenth century was Chief Toby Tubby. Tubby—whose name has been variously spelled as Tobba-tubby, Toba Tubba and Tobatubby—was the last Chickasaw chief in Oxford-Lafayette County. In the 1830s, he negotiated a peace between the two different Chickasaw tribes in Lafayette County, who were separated by the Yocona River. At the time, a particularly severe drought had decimated the game that the tribes depended on for food. The story goes that the chief of the southern tribe, accompanied by a farmer named Wolverton, asked the chief of the northern tribe, Toby Tubby, for permission to hunt on his tribe's land. Tubby gave them permission under the condition that they take no more than fifty deer on their hunt. By the time the southern tribe had completed their hunt, they discovered that they had killed fifty-three deer. To show their respect for Chief Toby's authority, the tribe gave the three extra deer to the northern tribe.

Chief Toby was also a significant figure in the white community. He became a rich planter and slave owner. He also operated a ferry across the Tallahatchie River. In 1835, Chief Toby sold several thousand acres of land. To celebrate the gold and government notes that he received in the sale, Chief Toby went to a saloon in Wyatt on the north side of the river. Fueled by large amounts of alcohol, Chief Toby became involved in a barroom brawl and was killed. Because the Chickasaw had assimilated with the Natchez Indians, Chief Toby was buried near his ferry according to Natchez customs, one of which held that a chief should be interred in a mound with all of his possessions and his slaves and relatives. According to tradition, Chief Toby was buried with the gold he had received in the sale of his land. In his will, he had requested that a slave be buried with him, but Chief Toby's white neighbors intervened.

The fate of Chief Toby's gold has been the subject of a great deal of speculation in Lafayette. Local legend has it that around the turn of the century, a woman claiming to be a descendant of Chief Toby's asked Charles and William Dooley for permission to dig into Chief Toby's burial mound, which was located on their property. The Dooleys sent a letter to the *Oxford Eagle* on September 1, 1895, notifying the editor of the woman's request. The story picks up again in 1972, when a resident of the College Hill community, Florence Dooley Tolson, revealed in an interview that her mother told her and her siblings that a strange woman arrived in College Hill to hire a work gang to dig for buried treasure. She promised to pay the men more than they would have received for working on a farm. Only one day after the dig had commenced, the woman vanished without paying the workers. The imprint of kettles and boxes was found at the dig site, but nothing else.

Many people in the College Hill community believe that Chief Toby's gold is still waiting to be found. Some say that it is still in the burial mound on the Dooleys' property. Others claim that the burial mound was probably inundated by the floodwaters generated by the building of the Sardis Dam. Chief Toby's burial mound was immortalized by author William Faulkner in his short story "Red Leaves," which includes the burial of a slave with an Indian chief.

THE LOST YANKEE PAYROLL (HOLLY SPRINGS)

The small town of Holly Springs played a pivotal role in the Civil War. On December 20, 1862, Union general Ulysses S. Grant was pushing through the interior of Mississippi as part of his first attempt to capture Vicksburg. Knowing that Grant could take his army only as far as his supplies would last, Confederate colonel John Griffith dispatched General Earl Van Dorn to capture the Union supply depot at Holly Springs. Van Dorn's cavalry captured fifteen hundred Union soldiers and destroyed approximately $1.5 million worth of Union supplies, seriously disrupting Grant's campaign.

The fate of the Union payroll is the focus of a legend involving a German immigrant named Herman Wohleben, known locally as "Ole Bully," who brought his wife to Ohio first and then to Oxford, where he worked as a blacksmith. Wohleben, his wife and their five daughters lived in rooms in back of the shop. In 1860, he moved his family to a cottage on Ninth Street. At the time of the raid on the Holly Springs supply depot, he was serving as a wagon master for General Van Dorn. In addition to supplies, large sheets of printed Federal banknotes were stored at Holly Springs. Each sheet measured four bills across and five bills down. On payday, the Union paymaster cut out the banknotes with a pair of scissors.

Amid all of the confusion during the raid, Wohleben helped himself to the Union payroll in the paymaster's office inside the depot on the east side of town. Legend has it that he made three trips back to Oxford with sheets of banknotes stuffed under his saddle blanket. After instructing his wife to bury the sheets in their yard, he hurried back to Van Dorn's army, which was moving across the Tennessee line. After the war, he was one of the few men in Oxford who had cash money. One legend has it that he deposited the cash in a Nashville bank. He is also said to have cut out banknotes from their hiding place every Thanksgiving. Many residents believe that Wohleben inadvertently assisted with the rebuilding of Oxford with Yankee money after the town was burned by the Yankees. The story of the German blacksmith who absconded with sheaths of uncut U.S. banknotes appears in William Faulkner's novel *Requiem for a Nun*.

THE BURIED TREASURE OF PATRICK SCOTT, THE IRISH PIRATE (OCEAN SPRINGS)

For twenty years, the pirate Patrick Scott was the scourge of Mobile Bay, yet surprisingly little is known about him. The Irish immigrant, who preferred to be called "Paddy," first appeared in Tuscaloosa in 1818, where he bought a forty-ton barge with the intention of starting a delivery business. No one knows for certain why he decided to embark on a criminal career instead. By 1824, he was a bona fide pirate. He and his ten-man Spanish crew stole a launch and preyed on ships in the Mobile area. When he and his crew boarded a British ship and stole food and liquor, he was using the alias

"Glass," probably in honor of the frontiersman Hugh Glass. In 1826, he and his partner, a brigand named Smiley, were using the Fowl River as their rendezvous point. At this time, they sailed in a small sloop, the *John Fowler*, which was heavily armed. That same year, the Revenue Marine, the precursor to the Coast Guard, captured the *John Fowler* off Horner Island and arrested Scott and Smiley. The buccaneers were not in jail for very long before they removed their manacles, knocked the jailer out and effected their escape out of town.

By 1827, Scott was operating around New Orleans in a small schooner called *The Fanny*. Scott soon abandoned *The Fanny* and commandeered another vessel, the *Lalla Rookh*, from which he and his crew prowled the Mississippi Sound. He took advantage of every opportunity to make a profit, regardless of its legality. When a group of visiting Charlestonians hired Scott to take them from Bay St. Louis to Biloxi, he and his men stole their baggage and set them adrift in a boat. He then turned his attention to the eastern shore, where he and his fellow pirates stole cattle. By this time, patrols from Pensacola, Mobile and New Orleans were on the lookout for the Irish pirate. Apparently, Scott was not intimidated by his wanted status in the least. According to the *Times-Picayune*, Scott brazenly walked down the streets of New Orleans, even though he had a $500 reward on his head in Mobile. Eventually, the police arrested him for vagrancy in New Orleans but turned him loose for lack of evidence.

On New Year's Day, 1840, Scott's crime spree came to an end. After stabbing a man in the back in New Orleans, he fled to Mobile. With a pale face and large build, the forty-plus-year-old pirate was easy to find. He was arrested in Mobile and returned to New Orleans, where he stood trial. Scott was found guilty and sentenced to hang by the judge. However, because of Scott's pathetic appearance, the jury asked the judge to spare the life of the aging pirate. The judge agreed and gave Scott a short sentence in jail. After his release, Scott spent the remainder of his life piloting boats on Lake Ponchartrain. His burial place is unknown.

Patrick Scott's memory is kept alive by the legend of his treasure. In his book *Legends and Lore of the Mississippi Golden Gulf Coast*, author Edmond Bourdreaux Jr. tells the story of a Frenchman and his mentally challenged wife and daughter who lived near the mouth of Bayou Portreaux. One day, the man's wife and daughter returned home with gold. The story, which was originally published in the *Biloxi News* on April 18, 1926, was told by eighty-five-year-old Captain Eugene Tiblier, who had first heard the tale from his mother. The newspaper article revived the old legend of Patrick Scott's buried treasure. Scott was rumored to have buried treasure in the mouth of Bayou Portreaux every four months. Captain Tibler told the reporter that people were already digging on his property before he purchased it in 1884. Tibler said that in 1890, a man named Barlow told Tibler to dig by an oak stump for Patrick Scott's gold. Captain Tibler dug at the stump and elsewhere on his property but did not find anything. According to another local story, an elderly man came to the property one evening and dug all night by the light of a lantern with no apparent success. If the legend is true that Patrick Scott and his crew really did bury their booty every three or four months, the treasure would be worth the trouble people have been going through to find it.

THE *BEN SHERROD* DISASTER (BLACK HAWK POINT)

Disasters are difficult enough to accept when an "Act of God" or nature is involved. When human error is involved, though, the loss of life is doubly tragic. A good case in point is the sinking of the steamship *Ben Sherrod* at Black Hawk Point, eight miles northeast of Fort Adams in Wilkinson County, Mississippi. In May 1837, the *Ben Sherrod* and the *Prairie* steamed out of New Orleans en route to St. Louis. Because the two steamers were keeping pace with each other at a rapid rate of speed, the passengers were well aware that the ships were in a race. To make matters worse, the crew of the *Ben Sherrod* were "fueled" by an open barrel of whiskey. By the time the ships reached Black Hawk Point, most of them were drunk after partaking of the free liquor for hours. The authorities who investigated the aftermath of the race ascertained that Captain Castleman of the *Ben Sherrod* was fully aware of the inebriated condition of his men. Suddenly, sparks ignited the resin-soaked cords of firewood. When it became obvious that the ship was on fire, the captain inexplicably refused to steer for shore until the tiller rope had burned through, making it impossible for the pilot to steer the ship.

Panic-stricken by the exploding gunpowder on board, the passengers, to escape their quarters, jumped into the river. At the same time, the boilers exploded, causing the *Ben Sherrod* to fold into itself. While a passing steamer, the *Columbus*, picked up some survivors, a number of them clung desperately to the blazing hulk of the *Ben Sherrod*, which drifted aimlessly down the river. Another steamer, the *Alton*, was not nearly as helpful as the *Columbus*. The captain of the *Columbus* shouted at the captain of the *Alton*, Captain

Dougherty, imploring him to rescue more survivors. Instead, Dougherty plowed over many of the people in the water. A number of the survivors drowned in the *Alton*'s wake.

Afterward, survivors and rescuers brought into focus the horrors endured by the innocent lives who were lost. Children and their parents were incinerated in their berths. Of the ten women who fearlessly jumped overboard together, only two survived. A man from Alabama who was clinging to a barrel hung on to a woman by her arm, only to have her drown as the *Alton* charged by. Mary Ann Walker, who had just witnessed her husband being burned alive, ripped off her dress and plunged into the water, holding her baby. The crew of the *Columbus* threw her a line; she grabbed it but was too exhausted to hold on for very long and disappeared beneath the waves. Because of the scores of lives that were lost, Congress passed stricter regulations regarding boiler use.

Aside from the morbid attraction that river disasters hold for many people, the sinking of the *Ben Sherrod* is especially important to treasure hunters because of the rumors that the steamer was carrying over $75,000 in gold. These stories acquired an air of credibility after several gold coins were discovered on the east bank of the Mississippi River near the community of Black Hawk. The *Ben Sherrod* is one of many nineteenth-century steamboats whose sunken cargo has become the target of treasure hunters, including the *Missouri Packet* (1820), the *Arabia* (1856), the *Twilight* (1865), the *Bertrand* (1865) and the *Leodora*. Attempts to bring their fabled treasure to the surface were thwarted in the nineteenth century by the absence of technological methodology. Hundreds of artifacts have been recovered, but no treasure, at least not at the time of this printing.

The possibility exists, however, that the *Ben Sherrod* has been found. According to an intriguing posting on jbcast at charter.net, the partially intact remains of a nineteenth-century steamboat were discovered near Fort Adams around 2014. The dig took place in a water-soaked field one and a half miles from the river. With the help of thirty diesel pumps and sheet pilings driven around the wreck, two feet of the hull were exposed above the water level. However, the project was abandoned following the accidental death of the leader of the project. No gold coins were discovered.

ROCKY SPRINGS' OUTLAW TREASURE
(ROCKY SPRINGS)

The remnants of the once-bustling town of Rocky Springs can be found in Claiborne County between the Old Port Gibson Road and the Natchez Trace Parkway at mile marker 54.8. The first white European to visit the area, a Spanish lieutenant, christened a spring "La Buente del Pedregal" ("Rocky Springs"). The town that developed here years later took its name from the spring. The first person to settle in what was to become Rocky Springs township was Mayburn Cooper, who arrived in 1796. He was followed by a planter and slaveholder named Isaac Powers, who built the Red House Inn, a popular stop on the Natchez Trace. The loosely connected group of settlers that eventually came here in the early 1800s grew in size. A Methodist church was built in Rocky Springs in 1837, and in 1838, the Rocky Springs Academy, where the sons of wealthy planters received their education, was established. Isaac Powers became the first postmaster. By 1860, the population had grown to 1,616 whites and 2,000 slaves. The farming community consisted of 54 cotton planters and 28 overseers.

The Civil War initiated the town's steady decline. When General Grant's army stayed in Rocky Springs on its way to Vicksburg in the spring of 1863, his troops lived off the land, taking most of the livestock and foodstuffs in Claiborne County. Yellow fever epidemics in 1878 and 1888 decimated the town's population. In 1905, an infestation of boll weevils destroyed most of the cotton crop in and around Rocky Springs. Rampant soil erosion amplified the farmers' problems. When the Rocky Springs post office closed in 1930, most of the population had already left. By 1940, Rocky Springs had become a ghost town. Only the 1837 Methodist church, the cemetery, the post office and a cistern remain. Rocky Springs is now a historic site supervised by the National Park Service.

Rocky Springs might have been completely lost in the historic memory were it not for its connection to the Mason-Harpe Gang in the early 1800s. Samuel "Wolfman" Mason was born in Norfolk, Virginia, on November 8, 1739. After rising to the rank of captain and distinguishing himself in the Revolutionary War, Mason bought a five-hundred-acre farm in Washington County, Pennsylvania. Rising debt caused him to lose his farm, so he moved to what is now Henderson, Kentucky, in the 1790s. His criminal career commenced after he moved to Diamond Island on the Ohio River. He and a gang of fellow criminals based themselves at Cave-in-Rock, where they robbed unsuspecting travelers

Very little remains of the town of Rocky Springs except for a few remnants, like this well. *Wikimedia Commons.*

who had stopped there for food and lodging. During Mason's time at Cave-in-Rock, he was joined briefly by the Harpe brothers—Micajah "Big" Harpe and Wiley "Little" Harpe—who were known in the region as a couple of cold-blooded murderers.

Mason's men were so appalled by the Harpes' method of throwing their naked victims off the top of a bluff that they asked them to leave. After being attacked by a group of bounty hunters, Mason and his gang relocated to the Natchez Trace, where they made a fortune robbing and killing unsuspecting travelers. In 1802, a posse tracked the gang to its hideout near Rocky Springs; by the time the men had arrived, the outlaws were gone. In 1803, Mason was arrested and tried by the colonial government in New Madrid, Missouri. Mason's possession of $7,000 and twenty human scalps convinced the jury that he was guilty. However, while being transported to the American governor in Mississippi Territory, Mason escaped, along with Wiley Harpe, with whom he had reunited. Governor William C.C. Claiborne offered $2,500 for Mason and Harpe's recapture. Not long thereafter, two men identifying themselves as John Setton/Sutton and James May brought in Mason's head to the authorities and tried to collect the reward money. However, they were recognized as Wiley Harpe and his accomplice, Peter Alston, and were hanged in Greenville, Mississippi, in 1804.

The Mason-Harpe Gang's reign of terror on the Natchez left an indelible impression on Rocky Springs. Supposedly, they buried thousands of dollars' worth of stolen silver and gold coins between the Methodist church and the cemetery at little Sand Creek. So far, no traces of the gang's treasure have been found.

THE COPELAND GANG'S LOST LOOT (CATAHOULA)

James Copeland is virtually unknown outside of the Deep South. Nevertheless, his exploits in some ways surpass those of the more highly romanticized American outlaws of the nineteenth century, such as Jesse James. Between the 1830s and the 1850s, Copeland and his gang cut a swath of crime throughout Mississippi, Alabama and Louisiana. He was born ten miles from the Alabama state line in Jackson County, Mississippi, on January 18, 1823. He was unruly as a boy, learning how to cheat and steal from his friends. Copeland stated that his actual criminal career began at the age of twelve, when he cheated a neighbor out of a pocketknife. Two years later, after Copeland stole fifteen pigs from the same neighbor, he was arrested by the Jackson County sheriff. His father hired a lawyer to defend him. Fearing that the lawyer would be unable to keep her son out of jail, Copeland's mother reached out to a thief from Mobile, Alabama, named Gale H. Wages, who believed that the only way to beat the charges of larceny was to destroy the evidence locked away in the Jackson County Courthouse. With the help of the older thief, Copeland burned down the courthouse and then fled to Mobile to join the Wages clan. His initiation into the group involved taking an oath of allegiance and learning the secret codes.

For the next two decades, Copeland and the Wages clan prowled around South Alabama and Mississippi, stealing private property and livestock, for the most part, although the sixty members of the gang also committed arson and murder, hijacked flatboats and engaged in counterfeiting. The members robbed the houses of worshipers attending revivals staged by one of their members, Charles McGrath. Copeland and his cronies specialized in the theft of slaves. After persuading slaves to run away from their masters, Copeland and his men resold them. One of Copeland's most heinous crimes involved impregnating a female slave he had enticed into running away with him and then selling her in New Orleans. The clan even set fire to the west side of Mobile and then sacked the east side in the resulting confusion. A few weeks later, the gang members burned up the east side of town so that they could rob the remaining houses and stores on the west side. The clan made its escape in boats in Mobile Bay.

Copeland's reign of terror came to an abrupt end in 1848. One of the clan's members, Allen Brown, took a $40 note on a farm and then sold it to James Andrew Harvey, who had connections to the Wages clan. When Harvey refused to pay the note, Brown arranged for Wages to take up the note, with the understanding that Wages would kill Harvey if he did not pay him. Wages and Harvey became embroiled in a heated argument over the note, and in the ensuing scuffle, Harvey killed Wages. Wages's father offered Copeland $1,000 to kill Harvey and take his scalp. With a $500 down payment in his pocket, Copeland and his men rode out to Harvey's farm. Harvey was not there, so Copeland and his friends roasted ears of corn while waiting for him to return. Alerted by the plume of smoke rising from his farm, Harvey and several other men snuck up on the intruders and started shooting. In the ensuring gun battle, Harvey and one of Copeland's men were killed. Copeland escaped, but he lost a map Wages had given him showing where he had hidden $30,000 of the gang's loot.

In the fall and winter of 1848, Copeland and his brother John made two trips to Catahoula to search for the money Wages had hidden away but were unable to find it. One day, Copeland tried to kill an Irishman named Smith who, he believed, was trying to arrest him. Smith drew a knife and stabbed Copeland in the collarbone. Copeland escaped to Mobile, where he was captured in 1849 and sentenced to a four-year prison term for the crimes he had committed in Alabama. Following his release, Copeland was transferred to Mississippi to stand trial for murdering Harvey. He was convicted of murder and sentenced to hang. While awaiting execution, Copeland dictated his life story to Sheriff J.R.S. Pitts. His hanging on October 30, 1857, was attended by hundreds of people, many of whom had traveled a long way to see justice served. Standing on the gallows, Copeland pleaded with the crowd to avoid fraternizing with "bad company." After the noose was placed around his neck, Copeland exclaimed, "Lord, have mercy on me." Spectators said that Copeland struggled briefly before dying. Pitts's book *The Life and Confession of the Noted Outlaw James Copeland* was published the next year. However, all of the copies of the first edition disappeared, prompting rumors that the Wages gang had vowed to steal all of the copies.

Copeland was buried near the Leaf River near Augusta, Mississippi. Three days later, grave robbers stole his body. A few months later, a skeleton purported to be that of James Copeland was displayed at McInnis and Dozier's Drugstore in Hattiesburg until the end of the 1800s. It disappeared in the early 1900s.

Tales of Copeland's hidden gold persist to this day in Mississippi. In 1884, loggers found a pot of gold coins on the banks of Red Creek in Meridian. This discovery sparked many attempts to locate Copeland's treasure within the bank. The banks of the East Pearl River in Hancock County and the Wolf River north of Pass Christian have been popular digging sites. Two other places where the gold is rumored to have been buried are near White

Harbor and near the site of Edgewater Mall in Biloxi. However, most treasure hunters believe that the Catahoula Swamp in Hancock County is the best place to search for Copeland's barrels of $30,000 worth of gold coins, primarily because Copeland himself said that this is where Wages buried the loot. Treasure hunters were still digging holes in fields and riverbanks as recently at 2010.

However, John D.W. Guice, author of *The Life and Confessions of James Copeland, the Great Southern Land Pirate*, is skeptical about the existence of Copeland's treasure. Guice believes that it would have been impossible to keep the location of the gold secret because of the large number of members in the Wages gang. "There may have been a little gold at some time, but I doubt very seriously that there was a great deal of it," Guice said.

8

LEGENDARY MURDERERS

MISSISSIPPI'S LIZZIE BORDEN (LAUREL)

In 1882, wealthy northern lumbermen, attracted by the area's abundant yellow pine forests, founded the town of Laurel. In the early 1900s, Laurel promoted itself as the center for the world's lumber production. Scores of displaced northern families fashioned a picturesque southern town out of the rural landscape, complete with churches, first-rate schools and a prosperous business district, as well as Mississippi's first art museum. In the 1930s, one of Laurel's most prominent families became the focus of one of the nation's most sensationalistic murders.

Ouida Keeton was the beautiful, intelligent daughter of one of Laurel's richest families. In 1935, when she was in her thirties, she was working as a secretary for W.M. Carter. She had gone to Washington, D.C., to take a hotel management course to fulfill her dream of opening up a hotel in New Orleans with her mother, Daisy Keeton. However, when she returned to Laurel from her studies, she began exhibiting traits of mental illness. One night, Ouida brutally murdered her tyrannical mother. She then dismembered the body, flushing some of the body parts down the toilet and burning most of the rest of the corpse in the fireplace. Ouida took her mother's legs, the only body parts that could not be easily destroyed, wrapped them in sugar sacks and drove then out to a lonely road north of town. Witnesses claimed to have seen her driving along the road shortly before the legs were discovered by a hunter and his dogs. Law enforcement officers used the evidence available to

The Lauren Rogers Museum of Art, Mississippi's first art museum, was founded in Laurel by the displaced northern families who were lured to the region by its yellow pine forests. *Wikimedia Commons.*

them to connect Ouida to the heinous murder. The motive for the murder was never definitively determined. Money certainly could have been a factor. However, people close to the family stated that Ouida's mother disapproved of her daughter's relationship with W.M. Carter, a much older man who was a successful businessman.

Ouida and Carter were tried in two separate cases. In the short trial that followed her arrest, Ouida pled insanity. Drifting in and out of consciousness during the trial, she implicated her former boss, Carter. The jury found her guilty, and she was sentenced to life in prison. Later found to be non compos mentis, Ouida died at Whitfield State Hospital in her sixties in 1973. The sixty-six-year-old Carter was charged with actually cutting up the corpse. Because the case against him was weak, he was able to win a new trial from the state supreme court. However, his case never came to trial because of Ouida's poor mental health. His life and reputation in tatters, Carter never fully recovered from the negative publicity, dying in his eighties in Laurel. In a bizarre turn of events, Mrs. Keeton's legs were given a full-scale funeral, presided over by the local Presbyterian minister. The legs were placed in a small box. To prevent grave robbing, the authorities buried the legs without a graveside ceremony. Ouida was buried next to her mother's remains.

In the years following the trial, the "Legs Murder Case" was featured in tabloids such as *True Crime Detective*, *Real Detective* and *Master Detective*. Ten years after the crime, national newspapers were still publishing feature stories about Ouida Keeton. Eventually, interest in the strange murder faded away until it was revived with the publication of Hunter Cole's *The Legs Murder Scandal* (2012). Questions still remain regarding the method used to dismember Daisy Keeton's body and the actual role of W.M. Carter in the crime.

THE CASANOVA KILLER COMES TO MISSISSIPPI (JACKSON)

When one thinks of serial killers, names like Ted Bundy, Richard Speck and John Wayne Gacy immediately come to mind. Less well known but equally horrendous are the murders committed by the person dubbed by the media as the "Cross Country Killer" and the "Casanova Killer." Glen Edward Rogers was born on July 15, 1962, in Hamilton, Ohio. His violent temper and contempt for authority were responsible for his expulsion from high school at age sixteen. He married his fourteen-year-old girlfriend, even though she had been impregnated by another man, but she divorced him two years later, accusing him of abusing her physically. He lived in Kentucky for a short time before deciding to drift across the county. Rogers was living in Southern California when police discovered the decomposed corpse of his roommate, seventy-one-year-old Mark Peters, under a pile of furniture in the cabin owned by the Rogers family in Beattyville, Kentucky, on January 10, 1994. On September 28, 1994, Sandra Gallagher, a thirty-three-year-old mother of three, met Rogers in a bar in Van Nuys, California. The next day, police were investigating a burned-out truck near Rogers's apartment when they discovered Gallagher's charred corpse.

The next stop in Rogers's killing spree was Jackson, Mississippi. In the fall of 1995, Rogers picked up Linda Price at a beer tent at the Mississippi State Fair. She was immediately smitten by the handsome stranger. Her sister Kathy Carroll recalled hearing her sister say, "Ain't he good looking?" several times. For a short time, Rogers and Price shared an apartment in Jackson. On Halloween night in 1995, Kathy Carroll suspected that something was wrong when her sister did not answer the doorbell, because Linda knew that Kathy's grandchildren were coming to her apartment for trick or treat. The next day, Linda Price's body was found in her bathtub at the Briarcrest

Apartments in south Jackson. She had been stabbed with a knife several times. Like Rogers's other female victims, Linda Price was in her thirties and she had red hair.

Rogers repeated his modus operandi on November 5, 1995, when he picked up Tina Marie Cribbs at the Showtown Bar in Gibsonton, Florida. On November 7, the maids at a Tampa Hotel discovered Cribbs's body in a bathtub. She, too, had been stabbed in the chest and buttocks multiple times. Later, Rogers's fingerprints were found on her wallet. When he was arrested on November 13, Rogers was sitting in Cribbs's car, drinking a beer. Two days prior, the corpse of an acquaintance of Rogers's, Andy Jiles Sutton, was found in her bedroom. Like Rogers's other victims, Sutton had been stabbed to death.

In 1997, Rogers was convicted in a Tampa, Florida courtroom of the murder of Tina Marie Cribbs. He was extradited to California two years later, where he stood trial for the murder of Sandra Gallagher. After he was convicted of murder and sentenced to death, Rogers was returned to Florida to serve out his prison term. Although Rogers is suspected of having murdered Linda Price in 1995, he was never tried in Mississippi, because he had already been found guilty of murder in Florida and California. Authorities believe that Rogers may be responsible for as many as seventy other murders across the United States.

Rogers's case took an odd twist in 2012. In a documentary titled *My Brother the Serial Killer*, Rogers's brother Clay claimed that Glen had confessed his involvement in the Nicole Brown Simpson and Ronald Goldman case in 1994. Glen said that O.J. Simpson hired him to break into Nicole Brown Simpson's house and steal a pair of earrings. Simpson added that Glen "might have to kill the bitch." Glen insisted that he, not O.J., murdered Brown and Goldman. Charlie Smith, who had investigated the Price murder in Jackson, does not believe Glen Rogers murdered Brown and Goldman. "I think he is just a psychopathic serial killer, and that is all there is to it, and he is trying to run his mouth, and he has lived way longer than he should have."

THE HORRIBLE HARPE BROTHERS (NATCHEZ)

The violent crimes of America's first documented serial killers began just as the colonies were shrugging off the shackles of Great Britain. The lives of Micajah and Wiley Harpe are cloaked in mystery, because many of the details are unrecorded. Although they were known far and wide as the Harpe "brothers," they were actually cousins. The Harpes were born sometime before 1768 in Orange County, North Carolina. Their fathers were Scottish immigrants. They assumed their nicknames while growing up, because Wiley was the smaller of the two boys. During the American Revolution, the Harpe brothers sided with the British, but they initially spent most of their time with a band of irregulars who raided colonial farmsteads, raping the women and stealing livestock, while the men were fighting for the Patriot cause. The Harpes became part of the regular British army in 1780, fighting battles in North and South Carolina. A Patriot soldier named Farak Wood reported seeing the Harpes serving "loosely" as Tory militia at the Battle of King Mountain in October 1780. Wood claimed that he shot at "Big" Harpe but missed.

In 1781, the Harpes joined up with a Cherokee raiding party, burning and pillaging farms in North Carolina and Tennessee. The brothers kidnapped a girl named Maria Davidson and Susan Wood, the daughter of James Wood, who had shot Wiley earlier while he was attempting to rape a girl. The Harpes, their "wives" and four other men traveled to Tennessee, where they took refuge in the Cherokee-Chickamauga village of Nickajack near present-day Chattanooga. During the twelve-year period when the Harpes lived at Nickajack, their women became pregnant twice. Both times, the brothers killed the infants soon after birth. The Harpes fought the British at the Battle of Blue Licks in 1782, one year after the British had surrendered at Yorktown.

When the brothers received word in September 1794 that the Americans were planning to attack the village of Nickajack, they fled to Powell's Valley in Tennessee, where they robbed the cabins of pioneers. Little is known of their exploits between the summer of 1795 and 1796. However, by the spring of 1797, they were living in a cabin on Beaver's Creek near Knoxville. On June 1, 1797, Wiley Harpe married Sarah Rice. His brother took up with two sisters, Sarah and Betsy Roberts. Big Harpe eventually married Betsy. The ceremony was conducted by her father, a preacher. Both women became pregnant. The Harpes were driven out of the Knoxville area later that year when the mutilated corpse of a man named Johnson was discovered in a river. His chest had been ripped opened, his entrails pulled out and rocks placed in the cavity to weigh the body down. This became the Harpes' standard method of disposing of the bodies of their victims.

The Harpes made their way to Kentucky on the Wilderness Road through the Cumberland Gap. In 1798, the Harpes committed a string of seemingly senseless murders. The brothers bragged about killing thirty-nine people, although many historians estimate the number to be much higher. The Harpes were accused of murdering a peddler named Peyton and stealing his horse and goods. After murdering two men traveling from Maryland, the Harpes were linked by an innkeeper with the death of John Langford from Virginia. The brothers were finally captured and incarcerated in the state jail in Danville, Kentucky, but they escaped. When they learned that a posse had been formed to return them to jail, the Harpes took revenge by murdering the son of one of their pursuers.

With a $300 bounty posted on their heads by Kentucky governor James Garrard, the Harpes headed north, killing two men, known only as Edmonton and Stump, on the way. Their destination was Cave-in-Rock in Illinois, the lair of the Samuel Mason Gang, a band of river pirates who preyed on flatboats on the Ohio River. Because the brothers enjoyed stripping their victims naked and shoving them off the bluff, Samuel Mason forced them to leave. Apparently, the Harpes' methods were too much, even for this band of cutthroats.

Cave-in-Rock in Hardin County, Illinois, was the lair of river pirates like the Mason Harpe Gang, which robbed unsuspecting flatboat men on their way down the Ohio River. *Wikimedia Commons.*

The Harpes resumed their murder spree in Tennessee. The first people they killed on their return in 1798 were a farmer named Bradbury, a man named Hardin and a boy named Coffey. For the next year, mutilated bodies seemed to be showing up everywhere. The disemboweled body of William Ballard turned up in the Holton River. James Brassel had his throat cut; his corpse was found on Brassel's Knob. The bodies of three men—John Tully, John Graves and his teenaged son—were discovered in south-central Kentucky. Someone had chopped them in their heads with an axe. The Harpes were also blamed for murdering a young female slave and an entire family while they slept in their camp. Annoyed by his infant-daughter's incessant crying, Micajah Harpe bashed her head against a tree in August 1788 near Russellville, Kentucky. A few days later, the Harpes gutted a man named Trowbridge and tossed his body in Highland Creek. During their overnight stay at the Stegall home in Webster County, the Harpes tomahawked a guest named Major William Love for snoring too loudly and Mrs. Moses Stegall's four-month-old baby, who had been crying all night. The mother screamed uncontrollably at the sight of her dead child. The Harpes then killed her, too. Most of these murders seemed to have been motivated more by bloodlust than by profit.

Moses Stegall, along with John Leiper, organized a posse to put an end to the Harpes' brutality. The posse caught up with the Harpes on August 23, 1799, just as they were preparing to rob and murder George Smith. The posse ordered the pair to surrender. Wiley Harpe ran off through the woods and got away. Leiber shot Micajah in the leg and back. As Big Harpe lay on the ground, paralyzed, Stegall walked up to him and began slowly sawing off his head with a butcher knife. Before he had cut all the way through the neck, Stegall twisted Big Harpe's head off his body. The outlaw's head was stuck on a pole and displayed at a crossroads that has come to be known as "Harpe's Head."

For the first time in his life, Wiley Harpe was truly alone in the world. He rejoined the Mason Gang at Cave-in-Rock. In 1803, Wiley and the rest of the gang were captured. Wiley and Mason got away, but Mason was shot in the leg. Little Harp then joined Peter Alston, who also went by James Mays. Wiley and the rest of the gang continued to prey on travelers on the Natchez Trace in Tennessee and Mississippi. For a while, the gang hid out in Rocky Springs, Mississippi. When a $2,000 reward was put up for Samuel Mason—dead or alive—two men calling themselves James Mays and John Setton showed up at the circuit court in Greenville, Mississippi, with Mason's head to claim their reward. One of the men in

Wiley "Little" Harpe and his gang preyed on travelers along the Natchez Trace in the early 1800s. *Wikimedia Commons.*

the courtroom, a Captain Stump from Kentucky, recognized the horses the two men had ridden into town on as his horses, which had been stolen in a robbery attempt. Pointing his finger, Stump exclaimed, "That's Wiley Harpe!" A man named John Bowman exclaimed, "If that's really Little Harpe, he'll have a scar under his left nipple on his breast, because I cut him there in a difficulty we had one night in Knoxville." Harpe's shirt was ripped off, revealing the incriminating scar. In January 1803, Wiley Harpe and Peter Alson were hanged in "Gallows-Field" in Greenville. Both men were decapitated. Little Harpe's head was stuck on a pole north of town; Alston's head was displayed in a similar fashion south of town. With the death of the Harpe brothers, people rode with more confidence up and down the Natchez Trace. The end of the Harpes' reign of terror ushered in a new chapter in the history of the Deep South.

9
MYSTERIOUS DEATHS

THE MERCRITIS EPIDEMIC (MISSISSIPPI)

One of Mississippi's most bizarre legends concerns a disease called "mercritis." Supposedly, mercritis infected the population of an unnamed small town in Mississippi and then spread throughout the state in the 1950s. The exact origin of the epidemic is unknown. Some people say that it was brought to Mississippi by European immigrants. The story goes that a man in a seaside village somewhere in Europe was chased by a dozen women down the street straight to the outskirts. When they reached the ocean, he plunged into the icy water, followed by his relentless pursuers. No one survived. Other residents of Mississippi believe that the disease originated in men who had ingested lead. The infection caused them to emit a chemical odor that transformed beautiful, intelligent women into homicidal maniacs. Armed with guns and kitchen knives, the "wild women" chased the men through the town, destroying everything in their wake. No one knows for certain how many men were killed in this outbreak of hormonal rage, because the government and the medical community conspired to cover up the strange disease for which they had no explanation.

Many folklorists cite the mercritis incident in Mississippi as a classic example of an urban legend. Rooted in modern popular culture, urban legends, according to folklorist Jan Howard Brunvand, "have a persistent hold on the imagination because they have an element of suspense or humor. They are plausible, and they have a moral." However, this possibly apocryphal disease is kept alive in tales told by older residents of the state to their children and grandchildren. The story also enjoys a second life on the internet. Mercritis affects less than one in ten million people in the general population. It strikes males of any age and is only contracted, as far as we know, from the oral consumption of certain types of paint. One of the reasons mercritis is rare is that paint consumption leads to massive organ failure, and many have a grim chance of developing the rare disease. The prevailing theory holds that the victim's skin, fed by secretions resident in the liver and kidneys, releases a mild odor that has an effect on women. Apparently, the only medical book on mercritis, *Mercritis, I Run* (translation), was written by Haruki Ryu, a Japanese doctor. Until more members of the medical community take the disease seriously, it will most likely remain within the realm of folklore.

WHAT HAPPENED TO JACQUELINE LEVITZ? (VICKSBURG)

Jacqueline Levitz was born in Oak Grove, Louisiana, one of nine children on a cotton farm. Following her high school graduation, she moved to Beaumont, Texas, where she lived with her sister Pat Tuminello while attending secretarial school. She was an attractive woman who won a beauty pageant shortly after arriving in Beaumont. Jacqueline married her first husband, Walter Bolton Jr., and moved to Washington, where she worked for a real estate office. Coworkers recalled that she had a talent for decorating houses before putting them on the market. Jacqueline had a son with her husband before their divorce. Her second marriage was to Banks L.O. Smith, a successful restaurant owner. After his death in 1968, she moved to Florida. Jacqueline's life drastically in 1987, when she was hired by furniture CEO Ralph Levitz to decorate his mansion in Palm Beach. Levitz had fashioned his furniture business into a $20 billion empire. Jacqueline and Levitz soon fell in love. She moved to his Palm Beach home, where she became a fixture in the city's social scene. When Jacqueline was not throwing elegant parties, she was devoting her time to charity work.

Jacqueline moved to Vicksburg following her husband's death in March 1995. By this time, she was a very wealthy woman, having inherited a trust fund estimated at between $5 million and $15 million. Jacqueline moved to a three-room ranch house on a bluff and immediately set about making improvements. She planned on adding four bedrooms to accommodate visiting family members. Her social activities were placed on indefinite hold while she supervised the work crew. In fact, she attended only one social event—a Mary Kay party—while living in Vicksburg.

On November 18, 1995, Jacqueline Levitz left her home to buy wallpaper in town. The store clerk who sold her the wallpaper was the last person to see her alive. Two days later, Nancy Whitten received a phone call from Tiki Shivers, Jacqueline's sister. Tiki said that she had been unable to reach Jacqueline by phone, and she asked Nancy to stop by the house and make sure she was all right. Nancy was surprised to find that all of the doors were locked except the front door. She walked into the bedroom, where she could hear the sound of the television. The bed was completely stripped; the bed comforter was rolled up and lying on the floor. At the foot of the bed was a dark patch of what appeared to be dried blood. Nancy entered the bathroom and immediately noticed that the frame on the closet was broken, as if someone had kicked it in. Nancy rushed to the kitchen and called Tiki Shivers's husband, James. She told him, "Things don't look good in here."

Shivers arrived a few minutes later with Paul Barrett, the county sheriff. A broken fingernail Barrett found on the bedroom floor indicated that Jacqueline had put up quite a fight. Barrett picked up the mattress and found a large bloodstain on the bottom. He concluded that no one could survive that much blood loss. However, Warren County sheriff Martin Pace, one of the deputies who had responded to the scene initially, disagreed. Members of the forensic lab and the FBI searched the house extensively that same day. A helicopter search conducted by the FBI found no signs of Jacqueline Levitz's body or the missing bedsheets, which may have been used to wrap up her body. One theory held that her body could not be found because it was thrown into the Mississippi River after she was murdered in her home.

In the months that followed, Pace's office received hundreds of tips, but none of them led authorities to her body. Cadaver dog teams, search dog teams and a series of aerial searches turned up nothing. Levitz was declared dead in a civil case in Florida in 2001.

WHO KILLED JANIE SHARP? (RURAL HILL)

In the early 1900s, Janie Sharp lived on a farm in western Winston County with her parents and her seven brothers and sisters. On July 21, 1910, Janie was a pretty eighteen-year-old who was engaged to a young man named Earl Ray. After helping her mother with dinner, Janie told her mother that she was going to the Williams' general store at Rural Hill to buy some goods and get the mail. Picking up her parasol and handkerchief, she set out on her one-and-a-half-mile walk to the store. According to some reports, she had intended to make a short stop at the home of Cyrus Ray, her fiancé's uncle, to do some dressmaking. She then set off for the store. Customers who were shopping there at the time recalled that Janie left the store at 3:00 p.m., carrying her parasol, her handkerchief, two letters and a copy of the *Weekly Commercial Appeal*.

When Janie did not return home later that evening, her mother left the house to look for her. Later that night, men from all over Winston County joined the search. Some people say that her father, Will Sharp, went to the circuit court's office to see if his daughter and Earl Ray had taken a marriage license and eloped. But Earl was in one of the search parties, so Will may have believed that she was involved with another man.

Most of the search party went home later that night, but her brother Lee Sharp continued to comb the area around Commodore Road. In the early-morning hours, he was climbing down a ravine when he discovered Janie's body lying by a muddy pool. Her head was submerged in the water. Lee was so shocked by what he had stumbled upon that he fainted on the spot. When he regained his senses, he started shouting for help. His father showed up a few minutes later and helped his son carry Janie's body home. Later that day, one of the members of the search party, Dr. W.M. Clemmons, examined Janie's corpse. In his report, he wrote that her throat had been cut from ear to ear and she had been struck in the head with considerable force by some kind of blunt instrument, like a pistol. Dr. Clemmons also noticed that Janie had been stabbed several times under the chin.

Meanwhile, Sheriff Hull and a group of people from Louisville arrived at the scene of the crime. All of the items that she had left the store with were scattered on the ground, except for her handkerchief. Tracks led from the road to the site of a struggle. Janie appeared to have been grabbed, dragged off the road and assaulted. More tracks indicated that she escaped and ran a short distance before being assaulted again. Evidence suggested that she might have gotten away a third time and ran back to the road, where she was killed.

One of the people standing in the crowd that had gathered outside of the Sharp family home after Janie's body had been found was a young man named Swinton Permenter. Later, people recalled that Swinton had been in one of the search parties and had discouraged the other searchers from looking into a patch of underbrush, claiming that he had already looked there. This was the place where Janie's body was discovered. He was also observed washing on the front porch after Janie's corpse was returned home. In the minds of many locals, Swinton's guilt was proven by a bloodhound named Ruth Hindoo, who led the searchers to the Permenter home. Concerned that Swinton and two of the boys he had been swimming with that afternoon—Alonzo Burchfield and Walter Cummings—would be lynched by an angry mob, the sheriff transported them to Winona. Rumors that Janie and Swinton may have had a love affair focused suspicion on Swinton, who was taken to Louisville to stand trial for the murder of Janie Sharp.

The trial was held in early October 1910. Swinton was convicted on mostly circumstantial evidence and sentenced to hang on November 25, 1910. On April 24, 1911, he was in the penitentiary in Jackson when the Supreme Court of Mississippi reversed the verdict. Swinton was released from prison and allowed to return home. His next trial was to be held in Winona in October 1911. During the yearlong interval, an investigator hired by the Permenter family, Ben Walker, was shot and killed by a shotgun blast at the home of Eugene Shumanker, who had filed an affidavit against Hulett Ray, one of the two men accused by Detective Ben Walker.

Swinton Permenter's second trial was set for early August 1912 in Louisville. Swinton's brother Walter, who claimed to have some important information collected by Ben Walker, was killed by a shotgun blast while filling a bucket with water at the pump. At the time, he and Swinton were staying at the home of Eugene Shewmake. Bloodhounds followed the trail taken by the assailant but lost the scent. Later, a boy found a shotgun with one spent shell in the cotton house. Some people believe Walter was killed because he resembled Swinton; others think he was shot because of the information he had received from Ben Walker.

Swinton's second trial was held on August 12, 1912, in Winona. Much of the prosecution's case was based on Swinton's possession of a woman's handkerchief. Swinton's sister Nellie testified that on the Fourth of July, she and several other young people attended a picnic at Indian Springs. Her brother Walter found a handkerchief and told Nellie to tell Swinton to try to find its owner. Apparently, Swinton could not find the owner or did not even try, which is why he had a lady's handkerchief in his possession. Nellie said that this handkerchief was identical to the one Janie owned. Closing arguments for the prosecution and defense were presented on August 22. On August 24, the jury delivered its verdict: not guilty.

After the jury's verdict was read, Swinton stood up and thanked the twelve members of the jury for acquitting him. Janie's father's reaction to the verdict was entirely different: "Nobody in the world but Permenter killed my daughter." Swinton was followed by court-appointed guards until he left Winona. The community was divided after the trial; most of the residents of the Rural Hill area were friends or relatives of the Sharps and the Permenters. Janie Sharp's murder was a "touchy" subject up to the 1950s, when students were forbidden to write about her death. Janie Sharp was buried in the Center Ridge Methodist Church cemetery east of Rural Hill. Her grave is marked by the tallest monument in the cemetery. For years, teenagers visited Janie Sharp's grave on Halloween night to tell ghost stories about her. At the time of this printing, her murder has still not been solved.

DEATH IN THE WOODS (PEARL RIVER)

When Norman Lander left his family's country store to go hunting on the afternoon of August 21, 1989, he was a happy seventeen-year-old, a fairly typical southern boy who loved being in the outdoors. His parents were confident in their son's familiarity with the woods and firearms, so they did not become concerned until he failed to come home later that evening. They conducted a thorough search of their property, focusing on the boy's favorite hunting spots. At 10:00 p.m., Norman Lander's body was discovered. He had been shot in the head. The sheriff's men examined the area where he was hunting and determined that he had fallen out of the tree and his gun went off when it struck the ground. The county coroner told Norman's mother and father that he agreed with the authorities that their son's death was a tragic accident. However, when he filed his official report, the coroner ruled the death a suicide. The bullet, he concluded, entered Norman's right temple and exited through his left. His parents vehemently disagreed, insisting that their son was not depressed and that he had no reason to kill himself.

Norman's father was convinced that the authorities and the coroner had jumped to a hasty conclusion. First of all, they assumed that Norman's gun was the one that was used to take his life. Therefore, the police did not fingerprint the gun or attempt to find the bullet that passed through his skull. The authorities also believed that the blood on a root proved that this had made the laceration on Norman's head. His father, however, said that Norman would have been forced backward after being shot in the head. Norman's father combed the area and finally found the bullet, which had traces of blood on it. The location of the bullet suggested that Norman was lying on the ground when he was shot. When the ballistics expert was unable to state conclusively that the bullet was fired from Norman's rifle and returned the bullet to Norman's parents, his father realized that this was not the same bullet that he had turned over to the police.

Three weeks later, Norman's parents went to the coroner's office to discuss their boy's official cause of death. While they were sitting in the waiting room, a stranger came up to Norman's mother and strongly advised her to drop their complaint, because their meddling could inadvertently endanger the lives of other children in the area. He added that their situation was hopeless. Norman's murderers would never be brought to trial. Undeterred, Norman's father returned to the site of his son's death and broadened his search. He was surprised to find some sort of radio device three hundred feet away from Norman's tree. The state authorities he showed the device to dismissed it as being irrelevant to the case. However, a DEA agent who looked at it told Norman's father that it was the sort of radio communicator that drug dealers used to signal pilots to drop packages containing drugs. The agent surmised that Norman had witnessed the delivery of the drugs or had recognized one of the drug dealers, who silenced him—permanently. On hearing the DEA agent's theory, Norman's parents recalled that Norman's wallet containing several hundred dollars, which was in his pocket when he went hunting, was missing. State authorities were not convinced that Norman Ladner was murdered by drug dealers.

The raft of unanswered questions swirling around Norman's case intrigued the producers of the television series *Unsolved Mysteries*. An episode focused on Norman's death was broadcast on November 21, 1990. Norman's father died in 2003, still certain that his son was murdered. Norman's mother and siblings continue to search for clues that will reveal the truth about Norman's death.

10

CEMETERY LEGENDS

THE GYPSY QUEEN OF ROSE HILL CEMETERY
(MERIDIAN)

The legend of Kelly Mitchell—"The Gypsy Queen"—began with her death in a Romani camp in Coatopa, Alabama, while trying to give birth to what would have been her fifteenth child on January 31, 1915. Her family decided to hold her funeral in nearby Meridian, Mississippi, because it would take an estimated twelve days for her followers to travel to the Deep South for the funeral, and Meridian had a refrigerator. Her body was kept on ice at Watkins Funeral Home until all of the gypsies arrived. The over twenty thousand Romani who gathered in Meridian camped all over the city in schools, parks, church lawns—any place that would have them. Many had arrived by special trains. The four tribes of Romani that made the trip to Meridian were the Bimbo, Mitchell, Costello and Marks tribes. St. Paul's Episcopal Church was selected for Kelly Mitchell's funeral. So many people were in attendance, though, that most of them had to stand outside the church. Music for the funeral procession was provided by a local college band.

Kelly Mitchell's burial at Rose Hill Cemetery is surrounded in myth. Over the years, people have said that the gypsies threw twenty-dollar gold pieces in her open grave. Consequently, vandals cracked the wolf stone covering her grave in an effort to find the apocryphal gold. Actually, custom

Following the death of Kelly Mitchell, the Gypsy Queen, on January 31, 1915, thousands of visitors to her grave in Rose Hill Cemetery have left coins, beads, liquor bottles, Orange Crush cans and other trinkets in the hope that her spirit will grant their wishes. *Courtesy of Marilyn Brown.*

dictated that mourners toss pennies, nickels and dimes in Mitchell's casket during the funeral, not gold coins. An article appearing in a 1942 edition of the *Meridian Star* claimed that Mitchell's coffin was made of gold and that Emil Mitchell was buried under layers of concrete twenty-seven years after his wife died. Neither story is true. Visitors to her grave have left Mardi Gras beads, cans of soda, bottles of beer and whiskey, flowers, trinkets, packs of cigarettes and assorted coins on top of Kelly Mitchell's and Emil's graves, in the hope that the offerings will compel her spirit to appear to them in a dream and provide answers to their problems. A number of other gypsies are buried next to Kelly and Emil. In fact, because of their burial, Rose Hill Cemetery has become one of the Romani people's main burial sites in America.

THE LADY IN RED (CRUGER)

Some of the most amazing archaeological discoveries have been made purely by accident. In 2016, construction workers were building a toilet at the Holy Trinity Church in Hildersham, Cambridgeshire, when they unearthed a huge Anglo-Saxon grave consisting of forty skeletons. In 2015, workers who were upgrading old water mains under Washington Square Park in Greenwich Village uncovered a nineteenth-century vault containing a number of skeletons. A similar discovery was made in Cruger, Mississippi, in the late 1960s.

In the summer of 1969, a work gang of farmhands was using a backhoe in a garden on Egypt Plantation when the operator heard a loud crunching sound. The workers immediately scrambled into the three-foot-deep ditch. What they found sent shivers down their spines—an old iron-and-glass coffin containing the corpse of a young, auburn-haired woman in her twenties. In the absence of a grave marker, dating the coffin was difficult. However, the girl was dressed in the fashion popular in the mid-1800s: a red velvet dress, a cape and buckled shoes. Her body was miraculously preserved by the alcohol that filled the sealed coffin. However, after the backhoe shattered the glass, the alcohol seeped into the ground, causing the body to deteriorate.

The mysterious "Lady in Red," as the young woman came to be known, was reburied in Odd Fellows Cemetery. The grave marker listed her birth date as 1835 and her death date as 1969. As a result of the publicity surrounding the workers' grisly find, her grave soon became a tourist

The tombstone of an unknown woman whose iron casket was discovered by a work crew on Egypt Plantation bears the approximate date of her birth and the year her remains were found. *flickr.com.*

attraction. Historians intrigued by the case were puzzled by the fact that she was buried in a location that was unoccupied at the time. One theory holds that she died while traveling as a passenger aboard a steamboat on the nearby Yazoo River. Some people believe that her coffin was hastily buried in a shallow grave because it had fallen off a wagon headed to the burial site. Researchers believe that the type of coffin she was buried in might also provide helpful clues. Almond Dunbar Fisk's iron coffins were often used in situations in which the deceased had contracted a communicable disease. The glass window enabled people to view the "dear departed" with no fear of contagion. Finding out where the coffin was purchased could provide information regarding where she was from and what the cause of death was. However, because it is unlikely that these documents will ever be found, the Lady in Red's true identity is likely to remain a mystery.

OLD ABERDEEN CEMETERY (ABERDEEN)

The town of Aberdeen was founded on the banks of the Tombigbee River. People began settling in the area in 1834, not long after the signing of the Treaty of Dancing Rabbit. Aberdeen was officially chartered as a town in 1837. By this time, people had been buried for several years in a plot of land that has come to be known as Old Aberdeen Cemetery, one of the most legendary cemeteries in the entire state.

An air of mystery hovers over many of the graves in the Old Aberdeen Cemetery. A number of the earliest burials are marked only by rocks with no inscriptions. Many of the graves in the confederate sections of the cemetery are unmarked as well. Aberdeen's Confederate monument, which was moved from its original location to make way for Highway 45, overlooks the graves of soldiers transported from the Battle of Shiloh. Some of these unidentified bodies could be the corpses of Union soldiers as well.

Aberdeen's best-known graves have stories connected to them. One of these graves is the final resting place of Graham McFarlane, who died on the same day as his oldest son. Etched on McFarlane's tombstone is a rambling rose bush with two roses lying on the ground beneath it. The two roses represent the father and son. The remaining roses on the bush stand for McFarlane's wife and remaining children. McFarlane's wife, who remarried twice, is buried separately. An even more bizarre tombstone marking the grave of a woman who burned to death depicts a female engulfed in flames. Without a doubt, the cemetery's most legendary grave is the tomb of Mrs.

The bodies of Confederate and possibly Union soldiers transported from the Battle of Shiloh are buried in the Confederate section of the Old Aberdeen Cemetery. *Wikimedia Commons.*

Needham Whitfield. Rumor has it that Mrs. Whitfield is sitting in her rocking chair in the tomb with her knitting in her hand. Generations of children living in Aberdeen grew up believing that on particularly quiet nights, they could hear the creaking of Mrs. Whitfield's rocking chair.

THE GRAVE OF ELIZABETH "BETSY" BELL
(WATER VALLEY)

In 1804, John Bell moved his wife and children from North Carolina to 320 acres of farmland in Adams, Tennessee. The Bell family's peaceful life was shattered forever by a number of strange events. Bizarre animals were seen prowling around the farm. Family members heard something knocking inside the wall and doors, chains being dragged through the house, rats gnawing on the beds and large rocks being dropped on the floor. After spending the night in the Bells' home, a neighbor insisted that a committee be formed to investigate the matter. Soon, word of the Bells' "family troubles" spread throughout the county, attracting curiosity seekers from miles around. The entity identified itself as a neighbor, Kate Batts. She stated her intention of killing John Bell. For three years, Kate Batts's spirit continued tormenting the Bell family. Her favorite target, aside from John Bell, was the youngest daughter, Elizabeth "Betsy" Bell. Night after night, Kate pulled Betsy's hair, scratched her back, pinched her arms and stuck her with pins. When John Bell died on December 20, 1820, most people believed he had been poisoned by Kate Batts. They also assumed that the malicious witch would leave his family alone following his death.

Unfortunately, Betsy Bell's life did not improve after her father's burial. While John Bell was alive, Kate Batts made it clear to the family that she disapproved of Betsy's boyfriend, Joshua Gardner. Because Kate had threatened to beat Betsy unless she ended the relationship, Betsy decided not to see Joshua anymore. However, the couple decided to start seeing each other again on Easter Sunday in 1821. Betsy and Joshua went on a picnic with two other couples. After lunch, Joshua and Betsy were fishing from a large rock on the riverbank when, suddenly, Joshua's fishing pole was yanked out of his hands and pulled into the river. At the same time, Kate Batts's spectral voice rang out, "Please, Betsy, do not marry Joshua Gardner." She repeated her plea two more times before fading away.

Betsy's fear for Joshua's safety drove her to break off their engagement. In an effort to keep Kate Batts out of her life, Betsy decided to marry her former

Located on the site of the Bell Farm in Adams, Tennessee, the Bell Witch Cave is said to have been the refuge of Kate Batts, John Bell's ghostly tormentor. *Wikipedia.*

schoolmaster, Richard Powell, in 1824, even though he was considerably older than she was. Powell embarked on a career in public life, serving as sheriff and as a member of the Tennessee legislature. The couple had a large family together. However, four of their children died young. One of their sons was killed in the Civil War. In 1837, Powell suffered a debilitating stroke. Betsy cared for Richard for eleven years before his death. Because he was unable to work, his family became destitute during this time. Betsy Bell Powell continued living in the shadow of Kate Batts, in spite of her efforts to leave that period of her life behind her. In 1849, she sued the *Saturday Evening Post* for publishing a story that asserted that Betsy Bell was actually responsible for the paranormal events in the family home.

After a few years, Betsy moved to Yalobusha County in North Mississippi to live with one of her children, Eliza Bell, and her son-in-law. Toward the end of her life, Betsy's health declined as a result of her weight gain. She died in 1888 and was buried at the Long Branch Cemetery in Water Valley.

Rumors that Betsy was still being hounded by the Bell Witch followed her to Mississippi. Even today, some residents of Water Valley believe that the Bell Witch is making it difficult for Betsy to rest in peace. Her original tombstone, which was heavily damaged by vandals, has been placed in storage. It was replaced by a more modern tombstone with an incorrect inscription. Unexplained events that have been reported around Long Branch Cemetery suggest that Kate Batts is not finished with the Bell family.

NATCHEZ CITY CEMETERY (NATCHEZ)

Natchez City Cemetery is one of the most storied burial grounds in Mississippi. Located on the bluffs overlooking the Mississippi, the cemetery was established in 1822 when remains from the city's first graveyard in Memorial Park were re-interred at the new site. Plots were sold for fifteen dollars apiece. The cemetery was divided into four sections: one for white people; one for people of color; one for Roman Catholics; and one for "strangers." Listed in the National Register of Historic Places, Natchez City Cemetery contains the graves of a number of historic figures, such as riverboat captain Thomas P. Leathers; General John A. Quitman, hero of the Mexican-American War; and Don José Vidal, governor of the National Spanish District. However, these important graves are overshadowed by the ones that are shrouded in legend and mystery.

The most famous monument in the Natchez City Cemetery is the "Turning Angel," which memorializes one of the city's most tragic catastrophes. On March 14, 1908, an explosion at the Natchez Drug Company took the lives of five girls, the youngest of whom was only twelve years old.

The Turning Angel Monument commemorates the death of five girls in an explosion at the Natchez Drug Company. Visitors to the Natchez City Cemetery say that the face of the angel turns toward them as they approach the monument. *flickr.com.*

Locals say that the mother of little Florence Irene Ford, who died on October 30, 1871, walked down the steps leading to the child's glass-enclosed coffin to comfort her during thunderstorms. *flickr.com.*

The owner of the company attempted to make amends by purchasing a plot for the victims and erecting a monument of an angel. The inscription on the monument reads, "Erected by the Natchez Drug Company to the memory of the unfortunate employees who lost their lives in the great disaster that destroyed its building on March 14, 1908." The sculptor designed the statue in such a way that when people drive past the cemetery at night and their headlights illuminate the statue, the angel's face appears to turn toward them.

The most mysterious headstone in the cemetery marks the grave of "Louise the Unfortunate." The headstone bears no name or dates. According to legend, she arrived in Natchez years ago to meet up with her fiancé. When she was unable to find him, she was forced to make a living through prostitution. Her grave plot and tombstone were purchased by an anonymous donor. In a sense, her grave commemorates the thousands of destitute people who have lived out their sad lives in Natchez.

A three-tier monument marks the grave of Rufus E. Case, who died on November 29, 1858. His plot is near the grave of a child in his family who died before he did. The story goes that Case was buried sitting in a rocking chair inside his monument.

The strangest grave in the entire cemetery is of Florence Irene Ford. She died of yellow fever on October 30, 1871, when she was ten years old. Her mother could not bear being separated from her child forever, so she instructed the workmen to construct a cement staircase leading down to her coffin. She was able to view the little girl's coffin through a glass pane. People say that because little Florence was terrified by thunderstorms, her mother walked down the steps leading to her grave and sat in front of the glass pane whenever dark clouds appeared in the sky.

THE WITCH'S GRAVE IN GLENWOOD CEMETERY (YAZOO CITY)

In the 1880s, Yazoo City was terrorized by a witch who lived on the edge of a swamp on the Yazoo River northwest of town. People said that she enticed fishermen to her house, where she tortured and murdered them. No incriminating evidence against her surfaced until one fall day in 1884. A teenage boy named Joe Bob Duggett was boating down the Yazoo near her house when he heard screams coming from inside. The curious lad peered through a window and was shocked to see an ugly old woman dancing and chanting around the bodies of two young men lying on the floor. The boy ran to the sheriff's office and described the nightmarish scene he had witnessed. The sheriff rounded up a posse and headed out to the witch's lair. The men chased her into the swamp, where she became mired in a pool of quicksand. As she sank into the muck, she delivered a curse on Yazoo City: "Everybody always hated me here. I shall return from my grave on May 25, 1904, and burn down the town."

Ignoring her threat, the men pulled her body out of the swampy water and buried her in an unmarked grave in Glenwood Cemetery. Although many citizens laughed at the possibility that her curse could come true, local authorities laid heavy chains on top of her grave just to make sure. Afterward, no one thought much about the witch's curse until May 25, 1904, when Yazoo City became a blazing inferno. Witnesses claimed that heavy winds seemingly propelled by a supernatural force spread the flames through the entire town. Every business and 200 houses burned to the ground. All totaled, 324 buildings were a total loss. Even though authorities traced the source of the conflagration to a fire in the kitchen of a Miss Wide, many of the survivors were certain that the witch's curse had come to pass. After the flames had died down, a delegation of citizens made its way to the witch's grave in Glenwood Cemetery. Most of the citizens were not surprised to find that the chains encircling her grave had been broken.

The legend of the Witch's Curse received national attention after the publication of Willie Morris's novel *Good Old Boy* in 1971. A marker was erected on the witch's grave in 1995, but it was smashed a few years later.

The best-known burial in Glenwood Cemetery in Yazoo City is the Witch's Grave. *Wikipedia.*

Interestingly enough, no one knows for sure who is buried in the Witch's Grave, because all of the city's cemetery records burned in the fire of 1904. Nevertheless, many people in Yazoo City still take the legend very seriously. On January 13, 2019, local media outlets reported that several of the links on the chains on the Witch's Grave in Glenwood Cemetery had been stolen. Not surprisingly, some people were concerned that the theft was going to unleash another curse on Yazoo City. At the time of this writing, Yazoo City is still standing.

ROBERT JOHNSON'S THREE GRAVE SITES (LEFLORE COUNTY)

The historical marker erected by the Mississippi Blues Commission states that Robert Johnson "synthesized the music of Delta blues pioneers such as Son House with outside traditions." Indeed, Johnson's music extends not only to blues artists such as Muddy Waters and Elmore James, but also to rock artists like Bob Dylan, Keith Richards, Robert Plant and Eric Clapton. His contributions to American music are inestimable. Ironically, no one knows for certain which of Robert Johnson's three reputed grave sites is the actual one.

All three of Johnson's reputed grave sites are in Leflore County, Mississippi. According to the Mississippi Blues Trail, he is most likely buried under a large pecan tree just outside of the Little Zion Missionary Baptist Church near Money, Mississippi. It is important to note, though, that the Mississippi Blues Trail marker states that "he is thought to be buried in this graveyard," suggesting that Johnson might be buried in one of the other sites. This tombstone is distinctive for the image of a note written in Johnson's own hand. The note reads:

Jesus of Nazareth, King of Jerusalem
I know that my Redeemer liveth and that
He will call me from the Grave

Another Robert Johnson grave can be found at the Payne Chapel Missionary Baptist Church in Quito, Mississippi. The U.S. National Park Service website's endorsement of this particular site as Johnson's grave is based on a supposed statement by David "Honeyboy" Edwards that Johnson's sister moved his body to Payne Chapel from Mt. Zion Missionary Baptist Church in Morgan City. However, in his autobiography, Edwards states that Johnson's sister had him exhumed, placed in a "decent" casket and reburied in the same plot.

The third reputed grave site can be found at the Mt. Zion Missionary Baptist Church cemetery. Supposedly, bluesmen Johnny Shines and Honeyboy Edwards] told Mack McMormic that he was buried in the graveyard of a small church near Morgan City. McMormic's research was cited in Peter Guralnick's book *Searching for Robert Johnson* (1982). Funding for the obelisk marking his grave was provided by the Mt. Zion Memorial

Robert Johnson was probably buried just outside of the Little Zion Missionary Baptist Church, according to the Mississippi Blues Trail. *flickr.com*.

Fund and ZZ Top. The titles of all twenty-nine of Johnson's songs are listed on the west side of the obelisk.

Adding to the confusion regarding Robert Johnson's actual grave site is his name. Many African American men in the twentieth century were named "Robert Johnson." It is possible, though not probable, that he is really buried in an entirely different location.

MASS GRAVE DISCOVERED AT THE UNIVERSITY OF MISSISSIPPI MEDICAL SCHOOL (JACKSON)

The Mississippi State Asylum, which was called the Mississippi State Lunatic Asylum for most of its history, was the state's first medical hospital. From 1855 until 1935, over thirty-five thousand patients were treated at the Jackson mental hospital. According to Dr. Molly Zuckerman, a biological anthropologist at Mississippi State University, "Mortality was very, very high [at the Mississippi State Lunatic Asylum]. Most patients died thirteen months after they were institutionalized." The primary causes of death were tuberculosis, heart attacks and strokes. Epidemics of influenza and yellow fever broke out periodically in the hospital. Nutritional deficiencies, such as a vitamin B deficiency (pellagra), also claimed hundreds of lives. Many of the nine thousand people who died in the hospital were buried on the grounds, either because their relatives could not be notified in time or because their relatives could not come.

The Mississippi State Lunatic Asylum closed in 1935. After its patients were moved to the new state hospital in Whitfield, the buildings were demolished, and the asylum became a fading memory. The complete absence of any tangible remnants of the old mental hospital accounts for the construction crew's complete surprise when workers unearthed forty-four unmarked graves during the building of new laundry facilities for the University of Mississippi Medical Center in the early 1990s. All of the pine coffins were unmarked. In 2013, workers uncovered sixty-six more bodies while doing road work on the campus. Once again, the pine coffins were laid out in neat rows. The next year, during the construction of a parking garage on a twenty-acre plot of land called Asylum Hill, radar scans detected the presence of over two thousand more bodies. The university estimates that as many as seven thousand patients may have been buried on Asylum Hill.

Researchers are learning a great deal from the 676 bodies exhumed in 2016. Tree rings in the wood in the coffins have revealed the age of the wood. Bacteria in the teeth has been analyzed to study disease before the advent of antibiotics. Thanks to the advances made in scientific and medical research, the nameless patients at the old Mississippi State Lunatic Asylum have finally been given a voice.

UNKNOWN CONFEDERATE CEMETERY ON THE NATCHEZ TRACE (TUPELO)

For most of the commanding officers of both the Union and Confederate armies, engaging and defeating the enemy was the top priority. Disposing of the casualties of warfare was often treated as an afterthought. Many soldiers on both sides were hastily buried in shallow graves where they fell. Even though protocol dictated that commanders require their soldiers to carry some form of personal identification with them at all times, few officers enforced this rule. As a result, approximately half of the Union soldiers and a much larger number of Confederate soldiers were nameless when they were interred.

No one knows why twelve unknown Confederate soldiers were buried along the Natchez Trace during the Civil War. *Wikimedia Commons.*

A sad reminder of the fate of some of these fallen heroes can be found in a lonely little cemetery on the Natchez Trace Parkway near mile marker 270, not far from Tupelo. The cemetery consists of the graves of thirteen unnamed Confederate soldiers. By the time of the Civil War, most of the Natchez Trace was no longer in use, having been replaced by steamboats. However, soldiers marching through northeast Mississippi probably did pass through the area where the Confederate cemetery is located. According to one theory, these soldiers died following the Battle of Brice's Cross Roads in 1864 or the evacuation of Corinth, Mississippi, that same year. Most likely, these were soldiers who succumbed to their wounds days or even weeks after the battles. It is also possible that they were taken, not by enemy fire, but by sickness and disease, which accounted for the majority of deaths during the war.

Sadly, most of the grave markers vanished in the first half of the twentieth century. In 1940, Senator Theodore Bilbo saw to it that marble headstones were placed on the graves. When these were vandalized and stolen, the National Park Service replaced them. Although the names of these soldiers may never be known, at least their sacrifice will never be forgotten.

FRIENDSHIP CEMETERY (COLUMBUS)

The Independent Order of Odd Fellows established Friendship Cemetery in Columbus on five acres in the shape of three interlocking circles. In 1957, the City of Columbus took over the cemetery, which had increased in size to thirty-five acres. In 1980, Friendship Cemetery was added to the National Register of Historic Places. Nine years later, it was designated a Mississippi Landmark. The long-dead occupants of the old cemetery are brought back to life every fall in the Tales of the Crypt tours, during which juniors from the Mississippi School of Math and Science take the role of people from the city's past. These historic figures are also given new life in the legends that people still tell about the cemetery.

Friendship Cemetery is best known as the birthplace of Memorial Day. Because Columbus had served as a military hospital center following the Battle of Shiloh, approximately two thousand Confederate soldiers are buried there. Local historian Rufus Ward estimates that at least fifty-one Union soldiers from Grant's army were buried there as well. On April 25, 1866, a contingent of ladies from Columbus decorated the graves of the Confederate and Union soldiers. Their selfless act inspired "The Blue and

The tradition of Memorial Day was initiated by a group of ladies who decorated the graves of Union and Confederate soldiers in Friendship Cemetery in 1866. *Wikipedia*.

the Gray," a poem by Francis Miles Finch. In 1867, almost all of the Union soldiers were re-interred at Corinth National Cemetery in Alcorn County. Eight of the Union graves remain unaccounted for.

Today, Friendship Cemetery is still in use, which is probably the reason why the old burial ground has generated so many legends. One of the most whimsical tales concerns Mrs. Munroe's white brick mausoleum. People say that if a visitor walks up the mausoleum and exclaims, "Mrs. Murone, what are you doing?" she replies, "Nothing." Variants of this tale can be found all over the United States. The most photographed monument in the cemetery—"The Angel of Grief"—marks the grave of Reverend Thomas Cox Teasdale. The statue's lifelike appearance has prompted some people to say that the statue's eyes follow them as they walk by. Others are "creeped out" by the flesh-like texture of the statue's arms.

By far, the most haunted part of Friendship Cemetery is the Confederate Soldiers' section. Many people have claimed to see the specter of a Confederate soldier patrolling the graves. On October 13, 2013, a page designer for a local newspaper, *The Dispatch*, may have had an "up close and personal" encounter with the spirits of one of the dead soldiers. Early one morning, just around sunrise, Matt Garner set up his tripod, pointed

Some visitors to Friendship Cemetery claim the eyes of the "Angel of Grief" monument followed them around. *flickr.com*.

it east and snapped ten photographs. He was trying to capture the way the sunlight filtered through the tree limbs. While he was examining one of the photographs afterward, Garner was unnerved by what he perceived to be the image of a ghostly face with dark, hollow eyes hovering over the ground. He was certain that he was alone in the cemetery at the time.

WORKS CONSULTED

Books

Blottner, Joseph. *Faulkner: A Biography*. Jackson: University Press of Mississippi, 1974.

Bond, Bradley. *Mississippi: A Documentary History*. Jackson: University of Mississippi Press, 2003.

Boudreaux, Edmond, Jr. *Legends and Lore of the Mississippi Golden Gulf Coast*. Charleston, SC: The History Press, 2013.

Brown, Alan. *Haunted Natchez*. Charleston, SC: The History Press, 2010.

———. *Haunted Places in the American South*. Jackson: University Press of Mississippi, 2002.

———. *Haunted Vicksburg*. Charleston, SC: The History Press, 2010.

Brunvand, Jan Howard. *The Vanishing Hitchhiker: American Urban Legends and Their Meaning*. New York: W.W. Norton and Company, 2003.

Conforth, Bruce. *Up Jumped the Devil: The Real Life of Robert Johnson*. Chicago: Chicago Review Press, 2019.

Daniels, Jonathan. *The Devil's Backbone: The Story of the Natchez Trace*. Gretna, LA: Pelican Publishing Company, 1998.

Davison, June. *Country Stores of Mississippi*. Charleston, SC: The History Press, 2014.

Fairley, Laura Nan, and James T. Dawson. *Paths to the Past: An Overview History of Lauderdale County, Mississippi*. Meridian, MS: Lauderdale County Department of Archives and History, 1988.

Guralnik, Peter. *Searching for Robert Johnson*. New York: Plume, 1982.

Hubbard, Sylvia Booth. *Ghosts! Personal Accounts of Modern Mississippi Hauntings.* Brandon, MS: QRP Books, 1992.

Lane, Shannon Hiurst. *Civil War Sites in the South.* Guilford, CT: Insider's Guide, 2007.

Lawless, Chuck. *Robert E. Lee Slept Here.* New York: Ballantine Books, 2011.

McCully, W.W. *Murder in Rural Hill: The Tragic Tale of Miss Janie Sharp and Swinton Permenter.* N.p.: Self-published, 2016.

Roth, Dave, ed. *Guide to Haunted Places of the Civil War.* Columbus, OH: Blue & Gray Magazine, 1996.

Sillery, Barbara. *The Haunting of Mississippi.* Gretna, LA: Pelican Publishing, 2011.

Internet Articles

Above Top Secret.com. "Policemen Witness UFO over Flora, Mississippi, 1977." http://www.abovetopsecret.com.

Alabama Music Hall of Fame. "Jimmie Rodgers." https://www.alamhof.org.

Al.com. "The Witch of Yazoo Still Haunts the Town She Burned." https://www.al.com.

And Speaking of Which. "The Bell Witch in Mississippi." http://andspeakingofwhich.blogspot.com.

———. "Helen Johnstone and the Chapel of the Cross." http://andspeakingofwhich.blogspot.com.

AP News. "Authorities Call in FBI, Doubtful Heiress Still Alive." Apnews.com.

The Atlantic.com. "The Plan for 7,000 Bodies Discovered Under a Mississippi Campus." https://www.theatlantic.com.

Atlas Obscura. "Grave of the Lady in Red." https://www.atlasobscura.com.

Bigfoot Field Researchers Organization. "Report #13494 (Class A)." http://www.bfro.net.

Biographies. "Elizabeth 'Betsy' Bell (1806–1888)." http://www.bellwitch.org.

Blackthen.com. "Was the Devil's Punchbowl a U.S. Concentration Camp for Black Slaves?" https://blackthen.com.

Church of the Redeemer. "Church of the Redeemer." https://redeemer-biloxi-dioms.org.

Civil War Talk. "Does the Ghost of Jefferson Davis Haunt Beauvoir?" https://civilwartalk.com.

CNN. "Katrina Uncovers a Little History in Mississippi." http://www.cnn.com.

Constant Contact.com. "Legs Murder Case." https://myemail. contantcontact.com.

Corpus Christi Rocks! "Galvan House Corpus Christi." https:// corpuschristirocks.com.

Daily Journal. "Something Strange in Your Neighborhood: Natchez Trace's Witch Dance." https://www.djournal.com.

Dark Destinations. "The Bell Witch in Mississippi." http://darkdestinations. blogspot.com.

Explore Southern History. "Ghost of Deer Island & Firewater Ghost." https://www.exploresoughternhistory.com.

————. "Mississippi's Singing River: The Mysterious Song of the Pascagoula." Southernhistory.blogspot.com.

————. "Unknown Civil War Soldiers." https://exploresouthernhistory.com.

Facebook.com. "Be Safe and Keep your Powder Dry." https://www. facebook.com.

————. "Haunted History-History & Haunting of Bellevue." https://www. facebook.com.

Faulkner Society. "Rowan Oak." https://faulknersociety.org.

Find a Grave. "Elizabeth 'Betsy' Bell Powell." https://www.findagrave.com.

First People. "The Little People: A Choctaw Legend." https://www. firstpeople.us.

Fox 10 TV. "The Alien Abduction: 45 Years Later, a Pascagoula Man Still Says He Was Taken by Aliens." https://www.fox10tv.com.

Ghost Stories. "Three-Legged Lady Road." Paranormalstories.blogspot.com.

Hancock Historical Society. "The James Copeland Gang." www. hancockhistoricalsociety.com.

Haunted Places. "Devil Worshiper Road." https://hauntedplaces.org.

Haunted Traveler. "A True Vicksburg Ghost Story." www.hauntedtraveler.com.

Hauntsofamerica. "The Haunting of the Chapel of the Cross." http:// hauntsofamerica.blogspot.com.

History. "Raid on Holly Springs, Mississippi." https://www.history.com.

Hottytoddy. "Buried Treasure Near Tallahatchie River." https://hottytoddy.com.

Huffington Post. "'Chupacabra' in Mississippi Town Reportedly a Coyote with Mange." https://www.huffpost.com.

————. "Up to 7,000 Bodies Found Buried Beneath University of Mississippi Medical Center." https://www.huffpost.com.

Jbcast at Charter.net. "[SEL] Fwd: A 150-Year-Old Steamboat." Lists.ceph.com.

Jimmie Rodgers Museum. "Biography." https://www.jimmierodgers.com/ museum.html.

KellyKazek.com. "Who Is Buried in 13 Mysterious Graves Along the Natchez Trace Parkway?" https://kellykazek.com.

KLTV. "Strange Creature Killed in Mississippi." http://www.kltv.com.

KRIS TV 6. "Ward-McCampbell House Heritage Park Corpus Christi, Texas 2005." (Halloween Special KRISTV6.) https://www.youtube.com.

KZRV 10 News. "Ward-McCampbell House Investigation with KZTV120news." https://www.youtube.com.

Lauchaussee, Alice Hill. "Longellow House." Mississippi Encyclopedia. https://mississippiencyclopedia.org.

Legends of America. "Confederate Graves on the Old Natchez Trace, Mississippi." https://legendsofamerica.com.

———. "Rocky Springs, Mississippi—Bandits and Bibles on the Natchez Trace." https://www.legendsofamerica.com.

———. "The Vicious Harpes—First American Serial Killers." https://www.legendsofamerica.com.

———. "The Witch Dance of the Natchez Trace, Mississippi." https://www.legendsofamerica.com.

Mental Floss. "Mississippi's Phantom Barber of Pascagoula." http://mentalfloss.com.

Merrehope. "Merrehope & F.W. Williams." www.merrehope.com/history.html.

Mississippi Blues Travellers. "Three Reputed Grave Sites for Robert Johnson in Leflore County, Mississippi." http://mississippibluestravellers.com.

Mississippi Encyclopedia. "James Copeland." http://www.mississippiencyclopedia.org.

Mississippi History Now. "Beauvoir." http://www.mshistorynow.mdah.ms.gov.

Mississippi Obscura. "One Legislator Has Never Left the Old Capitol." https://mississippiobscura.com.

Mississippi Sideboard. "Bellhaven's Haunted Beanery." https://jesseyancy.com.

Mufon. "Pascagoula Mississippi Case—1973." https://www.mufon.com.

Murderpedia. "Glen Edward Rogers." https://murderpedia.org.

Natchez Ghosts. "King's Tavern: The Truth Revealed." www.natchezghosts.blogspot.com.

National Park Service. "Nanih Waiya Mound and Village." https://nps.gov.

Newspapers.com. "The Phantom Barber of Pascagoula." https://blog.newspapers.com.

Newton County, Mississippi Historical and Genealogical Society. "The Chunky Train Wreck of 1863." https://nchgs.org.

Omgnews.today. "Horrific Unanswered Questions Haunt the Devil's Punchbowl Slave Concentration Camp." https://omgnews.today.

Only in Your State. "Crossing This Haunted Mississippi Bridge Will Give You Nightmares." https://www.onlyinyourstate.com.

———. "The Haunted Mississippi Theater Has a Bone-Chilling Past." https://www.onlyinourstate.com.

———. "King's Tavern in Mississippi Has a Haunting Past." https://www.onlyinyourstate.com.

———. "One of the Oldest Homes in the Country Is Right Here in Mississippi and You'll Definitely Want to Visit." https://www.onlyinyourstate.com.

———. "Spend the Night at Mississippi's Most haunted Campbround for a Truly Terrifying Experience." https://www.onlyinyourstate.com.

———. "The Story Behind This One Haunted Mississippi house Will Give You Nightmares." https://www.onlyinyourstate.com.

———. "The Tiny Town in Mississippi with a Terribly Creepy Past." https://onlyinyourstate.com.

———. "This Historic Mississippi Landmark Has a Haunting Past." https://www.onlyinyourstate.com.

———. "This Is by Far the Most Peculiar Mississippi Urban Legend of All Time." https://www.onlyinyourstate.com.

Parker Studios. "The Windsor Ruins of Mississippi." Sethparker.net.

Picayune Item. "Infamous Mississippi Murder Re-visited." http://www.picayuneitem.com.

Prairie Ghost. "Haunted Mississippi: The Deason House." http://www.prairieghosts.com.

Ranker. "12 Ghost Stories and Legends That Prove Mississippi Is the Creepiest State." https://www.ranker.com.

Rawls, Alan. "Nearby hauntings at Deason Home in Ellisville." Studentprintz.com. http://www.studentprintz.com.

Roadside America. "Lady Buried in Rocking Chair." https://www.roadsideamerica.com.

Roadtrippers. "The Longfellow House Is Believe Haunted by the Ghosts of Tortured Slaves." https://maps.roadtrippers.com.

S8int.com. "Mississippi's Prehistoric 'Great Wall' A Mysterious Structure Whose Builder No One Knows—Or a Natural Formation?" http://s8int.com.

Seeks Ghosts. "The Witch of Yazoo." https://seelsghosts.blogspot.com.

Smithsonian.com. "Thousands of Bodies Rest Under the University of Mississippi Medical Center Campus." https://www.smithsonianmag.com.

Smithsonian National Postal Museum. "Legend of the Singing River." https://postalmuseum.si.edu.html.

Southern Mysteries. "Episode 55: Who Killed Janie Sharp?" https://southernmysteries.com.

Suri, Charu. "Haunted Houses in Corpus Christi Christi, Texas." USA Today. https//traveltips.usatoday.com.

Sword and Scale. "The Phantom Barber of Pascagoula, Mississippi." http://sowrdandscale.com.

The 13th Floor. "Mississippi's Secret Diseaes the Government Tried to Cover Up." http://www.the13thfloor.tv.

Thought Catalog. "Here Is the Scariest Urban Legend from Every State." https://thoughtcatalog.com.

Unresolved Mysteries. "Norman Ladner." https://unresolvedmysteries.fandom.com.

———. "Who Was the Phantom Barber?" https://www.reddit.com.

Urban Legends Online. "Mercritis." https://urbanlegendsonline.com/mercritis.

Visit Vicksburg. "McRaven House: Vicksburg's Most Haunted Mansion." https://visitbicksburg.com.

WAPT 16 (ABC). "Flora UFO Sightings Remain Unexplained." https://www.wapt.com.

———. "Inmate Suspected in Jackson Murder Linked to Simpson Case." https://www.wapt.om.

WDAM 7. "Know Where You Go: Is There Hidden Gold in Perry County?" www.wdam.com.

WGNO. "Hometown Horror Jeff Davis Home." https://wgno.com.

WLBT. "Look Around Mississippi Brandywine Wall." http://www.wlbt.com.

———. "Old Aberdeen Cemetery." https://www.wlbt.com.

WLVT. "Deadly Tornado Devastated Hazlehurst 50 Years Ago Today." https://www.wlbt.com.

Writers Porch. "Haunted History at Rosswood Plantation." thewritersporch.blogspot.com.

Journals and Magazines

Capers, L.G. "Attention Gynaecologists!—Notes from the Diary of a Field and Hospital Surgeon, C.S.A." *American Medical Weekly* 19 (1874): 8–9.

Eveleth, Rose. "Pregnated by a Speeding Bullet, and Other Tall Tales." *Atlantic* 18 (November 2015).

Jones, Terry L. "Bigfoot: The Historical Record." *Country Roads*, March 5, 2018.

Sledge, John. "Paddy Scott." *Mobile Bay*, December 7, 2018.

Taylor, Courtney. "Haunted Natchez." *Country Roads*, September 1, 2014.

Newspapers

Apel, Therese. "Bigfoot, Seriously? 2 Vicksburg Men Aren't Playing." *Clarion-Ledger*, September 1, 2014.

———. "Reports: Spirits Speak at Ellisville's Deason Home." *Clarion-Ledger*, October 28, 2014.

Barnett, Sheena. "Summoning Antoine: Haunted Theatre Brings Up Scary Memories." *Daily Journal* (Tupelo, MS), October 9, 2014.

Bloom, Brian. "'No One to Pray Over Her.' Unearthed in 1969, Lady in Red Remains a Mystery." *Clarion-Ledger*, February 17, 2019.

Boon, Catherine. "The Legend of 'Ole Bully' Wohleben and the Yankee Payroll." *Oxford (MS) Eagle*, December 4, 2016.

Broom, Brian. "5 Scariest Things in the Mississippi Woods." *Clarion-Ledger*, October 14, 2014.

———. "'The Story Is Very True. That's What Has Bothered Me for 45 Years.' UFO Witnesses Speak." *Clarion-Ledger*, March 14, 2019.

Browning, Willikam. "Ghosts of Columbus: With Halloween Upon Us, a Look at Area Hauntings." *The Dispatch* (Columbus, MS), October 31, 2013.

Ciurczak, Ellen. "Did a Bullet Impregnate a Woman in the Civil War? New Film Tells the Tale." *Clarion-Ledger*, March 27, 2019.

Clarion-Ledger. "Hundreds of UFO Sightings Reported in Mississippi." July 2, 2014.

Fowler, Sarah. "Mississippians Share Bigfoot Stories. *Clarion-Ledger*, January 18, 2016.

Gaffey, Jan. "Socialite's Death Remains Unsolved 20 Years Later." *Vicksburg (MS) Post*, December 6, 2015.

Jacob, Jennifer. "Ghost Dog Guards Historic Store." *Meridian (MS) Star*, October 30, 2011.

———. "The Hanging Man at Stuckey's Bridge." *Meridian Star*, October 28, 2007.

————. "Merrehope: Meridian's Haunted Mansion." *Meridian Star*, October 28, 2007.

————. "Queen Kelly Mitchell; A Slice of Meridian's History." *Meridian Star*, December 25, 2007.

"Killer Found Guilty in 2nd Murder Case." *Los Angeles Times*, June 23, 1999.

Minor, Bill. "Ouida Lives Again in 'The Legs Murder Scandal.'" *Desoto (MS) Times*, September 29, 2010.

"MSU library, Ole Miss Anthropologist, Local Historian Search for Union Graves." *Clarion-Ledger*, May 27, 2018.

Nelson, Stanley. "Terror Aboard the *Ben Sherrod*." *Catahoula News Booster*. June 26, 2019.

Russell, W. Derek. "Something Strange in Your Neighborhood: Oxford's Rowan Oak." *Daily Journal*. https://djournal.com.

————. "Something Strange in Your Neighborhood: Tupelo's Lyric Theatre." *Daily Journal*, October 7, 2016.

Watkins, Billy. "Mississippi 13th Most Likely State to See UFO and This Writer Saw One." *Clarion-Ledger*, October 4, 2018.

Zhu, Alissa. "Mystery of Hazlehurst: Boy 'Prophet' Warned of a Tornado 50 Years Ago, Then Disappeared." *Clarion-Ledger*, January 23, 2019.

Documents

National Register of Historic Places Registration Form. Old Mississippi State Capitol. Retrieved January 16, 2020.

National Register of Historic Places Inventory—Nomination Form. Rosswood Plantation. Retrieved January 18, 2020.

————. The Old Capitol. Retrieved January 16, 2020.

Interviews

Johnson, Faye. Personal interview, January 8, 2020.

Rush, Fonda. Personal interview, December 12, 1995.

ABOUT THE AUTHOR

Alan Brown teaches English at the University of West Alabama in Livingston, Alabama. A transplanted Yankee from Alton, Illinois, Alan has written primarily about southern ghost lore, a passion that his taken him to haunted places throughout the entire Deep South, as well as parts of the Midwest and the Southwest. As a rule, his wife, Marilyn, accompanies him on these trips and occasionally serves as his "ghost magnet" when they spend the night at haunted hotels and bed-and-breakfasts. Some of her encounters with the spirit world have been incorporated in a number of Alan's books. In 2018, Alan decided to explore another abiding interest of his—mysteries and legends—in books like *Eerie Alabama* and *The Unexplained South*. When he is not teaching or writing, Alan is watching old movies, reading thrillers and playing with his two grandsons, Cade and Owen, who keep him young.

Visit us at
www.historypress.com